Regifting Revival!

Regifting Revival!

A Guide to Reusing Gifts Graciously

Jodi Newbern

Synergy Books

Regifting Revival!: A Guide to Reusing Gifts Graciously
Published by Synergy Books
P.O. Box 80107
Austin, TX 78758

For more information about our books, please write to us, call 512.478.2028, or visit our website at www.synergybooks.net

Newbern, Jodi.
    Regifting revival! : a guide to reusing gifts
graciously / Jodi Newbern.
      p. cm.
      LCCN 2008910437
      ISBN-13: 978-0-9815462-9-2
      ISBN-10: 0-9815462-9-3

      1. Gifts.   I. Title.

GT3040.N49 2009   394
                                QBI08-600332

Illustrations by Dee Densmore-D'Amico
Cover by James Jensen

Please visit RegiftingRevival.com for more tips and ideas and to share your regifting stories.

10 9 8 7 6 5 4 3 2 1

To my parents, my siblings, and my wonderful family and friends,

to my amazing children, Amanda and Kevin,

and to my husband and best friend, Lorenzo.

(Remember, it's all part of His plan...)

Table of Contents

"Love means never having to say you're sorry you regifted."

~regifting proverb

Introduction

Usually people have little or no problem purchasing used or "previously owned" cars, clothes, videos, appliances, sports equipment, furniture, and pets. However, for some reason (which we will discuss here), when you give someone a previously owned gift, or regift, even if it was not "previously used" at all by anyone, people tend to find that somewhat insulting, inconsiderate, and sometimes even extremely tacky.

It has been said that you should only write about what you know. If that's true, then there should be no question as to why I wrote this book. As far back as I can remember, regifting has been a popular gift-giving option in my family. We never named it; we just did it, any time an opportunity arose. We figured, I guess, that if you got a gift from someone that you couldn't use, didn't like, or didn't really want, the only right thing to do was to go ahead and give that gift to someone else, especially if you knew the "gift getter" would appreciate it (or, at least, that's what we thought). We never thought of it as being in poor taste. On the contrary, many of our most memorable gift-giving and gift-getting moments resulted from regifting, although much of the time it was done with a sense of humor and good will. It wasn't until our "unique" gift-giving methods extended to others outside of our family, and the "buying" of gifts was expected, that the concept of regifting became a debatable and quite controversial matter. It is still that way for most people, especially among those getting the regifts.

Because of extreme reluctance on the part of the majority of people to even consider regifting a viable alternative in the giving of gifts (surely due, in part, to so much negative hype in the past), I intend to reintroduce to the world the essentially lost art of regifting and the rudimentary role it can play in our economic future. Frankly, with global warming, there is a critical need for us to reuse and recycle as much as we can. With resources becoming scarcer and the economy becoming rockier, now is the time for regifting to be resurrected as a wonderful, wise, and responsible way for all of us to fight against the continued waste of unwanted gifts! I want to educate others about the importance of bringing back the fine art of regifting, since it is clearly a great way to overcome some of these issues. Regifting should become the obvious choice when choosing to give someone a gift for any reason, and so we need to bring about a regifting revival! No matter what opinion you previously held about regifting, this guide will get you thinking outside the regift box and show you how thoughtful and rewarding regifting can be. No longer will you consider regifting to be tacky and cheap and only an option for ignorant gift givers trying to unload their own tasteless stuff onto other people. Instead, you will realize regifting is truly creative, clever, and classy, and you will have learned everything you need to know to be able to regift properly.

And not just regift, but *graciously* regift, which, as you will learn here, takes regular regifting to a much higher level. Giving great gifts no longer has to take a big bite out of your budget, but neither will spending less money keep you from coming up with cool gifts you can proudly give to anyone. Now you will finally have a way to recycle all of those unwanted gifts that have been cluttering up your drawers and closets.

This book will be your definitive source for all things regiftable. We'll cover the basics of gift giving, discover why regifting has such a bad rap, break down the different types of gifts and how to regift them graciously, and wrap up with some last tips on how to ensure total regifting success. After reading it, you should be a regifting pro, but just in case you need a few reminders, keep this guide handy so you can refer back to it again and again.

"Tis a gift to be simple, 'tis a regift to be free."

~Irish regifting proverb

The Art of Gift Giving
What Gives?

1

So you have to give someone a gift. Are you up to the challenge? If you already feel certain that your gift-giving prowess is reputable and indisputable, then after reading this book, you will have even more options to express your creativity when deciding on the perfect gift to give. Or maybe you are the type of gift giver who just wants the gift to be something simple, painless, and as inexpensive as possible. Then, of course, generic gifts, such as gift cards, gift certificates, and cold, hard cash are always an option for you, but after reading this book, you will see that sometimes there is nothing more "simple, painless, and inexpensive" than regifting.

On the other hand, if you are the kind of person who, when gift giving is mandatory, is (a) completely clueless about the process, (b) extremely annoyed by the whole idea, or (c) totally open to any possibilities that would get you giving an awesome gift, then this book will be your salvation. We promise you will see how almost anyone can become a Gracious Regifter!

However, before we get down to the nuts and bolts of regifting, let's take a moment to review some of the basic principles of giving a great gift, to anyone for any reason. If you are already an experienced gift giver, you might wish to skip ahead to the section "To Gift or to Regift: That Is the Question." But if you consider yourself a gifting novice, then read on, my friend! Let us show you how it's done.

Gift Giving Is Fundamental

There is a certain finesse to gift giving. *What* you are giving can actually be less important than *why* you are giving it, and *how* you give the gift is almost as significant as to *whom* you give the gift. There are very fine gift givers who put time, trouble, thought, and effort into the gifts that they give (whether new gifts or regifts), and then there are those who simply give gifts without any thought to what might be more appropriate for the person or the occasion.

At the most basic level, to be a savvy gift giver, you need to consider three things when choosing any type of gift: you need the right gift for the right person, the right gift for the right occasion, and the right gift for the right price.

Considering all three elements can make a big difference to a gift's overall impact. This is important to note because choosing to give a too elaborate gift can be just as inappropriate as giving a gift that is too chintzy.

The Right Person: Determining Who's Giving and Who's Getting

Research done by the Gift Appreciation Group (GAG) shows there are four typical types of gift givers and four types of typical gift getters. Having a good understanding of what kind of a gifter you are, as well as the type of giftee you will be giving a gift to, is important when you are deciding on how best to complete the gift-giving experience. Let's examine the differences between the types of givers and getters, as some of them are quite subtle, as well as some examples of each.

Which one are you?

Generous Gift Giver

You truly enjoy giving gifts—for whatever reason, whatever the occasion, and no matter whom it is for. You like to give people presents "just because." You can always find a reason to give someone a gift, so you do—often and a lot. And you always have a good reason for it, too, no matter how ridiculous it may seem to someone else.

⊙ **Example**: "Here's a little something I picked out for you since you have been so nice to my hamster."

⊙ **Regifter potential:** The Generous Gift Giver is definitely a potential regifter in order to afford all of those presents!

Gratuitous Gift Giver

You are similar to the Generous Gift Giver; however, as a Gratuitous Gift Giver, you feel the need to give gifts of appreciation, thanks, recognition, affection…to everyone for everything. You always feel indebted to someone for some reason and feel an overwhelming need to "repay" someone somehow for whatever it is that they have done. This obligation also extends to situations where gifts are not required, and possibly even prohibited, yet you still feel the need to give *something*. Attending any occasion or function empty-handed is against your law. For example, bringing a three-course, homemade meal to a casual cocktail party. (This last type of gratuitous gift giving is usually only a dilemma for women. Most men never seem to feel any guilt or type of obligation to bring anything to someone's house, especially if told not to, no matter how much of their hosts' food and beer they consume…) Depending on the severity of your sense of obligation, you might even feel the need to give a gift just for receiving a gift.

⊙ **Example**: "I hope you like this—I wanted to thank you for the wedding gift you sent."

⊙ **Regifter potential:** Since the Gratuitous Gift Giver has so many opportunities to show their appreciation, they could have a really good reason for wanting to regift.

Forgetful Gift Giver

You are the kind of person who doesn't remember it's your friend's birthday until someone asks, "Are you going to the party tonight?" Alternatively, you're the kind of person who procrastinates on buying a gift until five minutes before you need to leave for the party (which you've known about for weeks). As a result, you're always scrambling, sometimes in a panic, to put together a gift or gifts for any and all occasions at the last minute. (Since you must do well under pressure, holiday shopping is no exception!)

⊙ **Example**: "I bought your gift, like, a month ago. I'm only late because my car happened to break down in front of the mall."

⊙ **Regifter potential:** These are the types of people who will try to find anything to give, usually at the zero hour, and are actually somewhat capable of creating really cool stuff out of their own stash, if they have the time. Having a dedicated stock of regiftable items can really help cut down on stress and can even boost the quality of the gift.

Grudging Gift Giver

You know who you are. First off, you hate giving gifts—to anyone, for any occasion. The whole idea of giving a gift to anybody for any reason is very distasteful to you, although the need to dole out some of your hard-earned dollars is usually the only issue. Due to your reputation, it's doubtful that anyone, not even your relatives, expects to be dazzled by your gift giving anyway, so you don't suffer from the stress of their potential disappointment. More often than not, you will probably try to pawn your gift-giving duties off to someone else, most likely a spouse or other family member. (However, I would bet that you still have some kind of opinion about whatever gift eventually was chosen to give…)

⊙ **Example:** "Why do we have to give them a gift? Why do we always have to give everyone a gift? Why don't you just buy them a car?"

(Sarcasm aside, some of you Grudging Gift Givers usually are very agreeable to *getting* gifts…)

⊙ **Regifter potential:** The Grudging Gift Givers are obviously the very dolts who helped drag the idea of regifting down to its current infamy. To them, regifting is simply a quick fix to an annoying problem, and probably not one moment of thought is expended to make the regift something great.

Genial Gift Getter

You absolutely *love* every single gift you get—no matter what it is or whom it's from! You make every gift giver, no matter what type, feel as if his or her gift is the best gift you have ever received. You make them all feel special (and possibly a little guilty, especially if they did not put much thought into the gift). You also always make a sincere effort to use the gift you have received, which can lead to an eclectic décor and a *lot* of useless knickknacks.

> ◉ **Example**: "I *love* these dryer balls! How did you know I've been looking all over for them?"

> ◉ **Regiftee potential:** The Genial Gift Getter is a good candidate for *getting* a regift, since most likely every gift received is used or displayed immediately, saved for future use, or stored away forever. (Unfortunately, he or she is probably quite reluctant to part with any of them as a potential regifter.)

Grateful Gift Getter

You will say thank you. And thank you. And thank you again—over and over until the gift giver wishes he hadn't even given you a gift in the first place, or that he had given you something a little less "extraordinary!" Really, though, it doesn't matter what it was, because as a Grateful Gift Getter, you are grateful for *every* gift, no matter what it is. Unlike the Genial Gift Getter, you never actually announce your affections for the gift, only your gratitude for getting it. Therefore, the gift giver really cannot figure out your real feelings for it—he just has to watch for what you do with it after you receive it…

- ◉ **Example**: "Is this for me? Really? Thank you! I cannot believe you got me this! Wow! Thank you so much!"

- ◉ **Regiftee potential**: Since a Grateful Gift Getter is so (overly) grateful for any gift, whether she will ever use it or not, the Grateful Gift Getter will always seem thankful for a regift. However, because it's hard to tell whether she really liked the gift or just the gesture, you'll have to utilize your gracious regifting skills to ensure a true regifting success.

Greedy Gift Getter

You know who you are. You get a nice gift, feign some automatic expression of appreciation, and then, seriously, ask The Question (or something as equally obnoxious).

- ◉ **Example**: "Thanks…Is that all?"

Normally one might assume that this declaration of astonishment would only be uttered by totally clueless people (or spoiled kids), but the truth is, arguably, that some of you Greedy Gift Getters never learned the importance of showing appreciation for any and all gifts you get. You never get what you really wanted, or asked for, what you deserve, or what you feel is fair. For a Greedy Gift Getter, enough is never enough. You want more or, conceivably, even something else entirely. You may also appear angry or annoyed with the gift you get. You may seem disappointed and may even pout because you didn't get what you wanted. (Although the Greedy Gift Getter may not yet consider regifting because they usually will either return their unwanted gift, or just throw it out, they may soon realize that regifting could relieve them of some terrific regiftable stuff.)

- ⦿ **Regiftee potential:** Since they never seem to be satisfied with "just enough" and always want "a little more," regifting to the Greedy Gift Getter is a good idea, if only to try to keep a lid on your budget since it probably won't matter much anyway!

Grumbling Gift Getter

Cousin to the Greedy Gift Getter, as a Grumbling Gift Getter, you are just genuinely unappreciative of *any* gift, even if the gift is actually what you wanted and asked for in the first place. There is apparently no pleasing you, no matter how hard the gift giver tried to find the perfect present, and no matter how great or significant the stupid gift even is. Maybe it can be traced back to some early gift-getting trauma. However, the giver will probably never know because even if you mumble some semblance of satisfaction, it will still be evident that whatever it was you were given is somehow wrong in some way.

⊙ **Example**: "What's this—a widget for my workbench? It's not the one I wanted. This one is way too wide. But—thanks..." ("Do you have the receipt?")

Note: Prior to a proper gift-getting occasion, the Grumbling Gift Getter may even utter innocuous insinuations such as "no gift is necessary," or "don't get me anything..." Unfortunately, for the potential gift giver, woe be to you if you abide by their wish and forego the gift entirely.

⊙ **Regiftee potential:** Realize that there are those gift givers who will go to great lengths to find *the* right gift for every gift getter, no matter which type they are. They seem to look at it as a challenge, wanting to be the one who receives genuine appreciation from the Grumbling Gift Getter for their chosen gift. In that case, if the perfect present happens to be a regift, then go ahead and graciously regift it. What do you have to lose?

Most likely, you have recognized yourself, someone you know, and probably all of your relatives in these categories. You may even have jotted down names next to the most suitable descriptions for future reference.

In any case, now we have defined the identities and established the unique characteristics of all types of gift givers and gift getters. Obviously, there are "normal" gift givers and getters who fall somewhere in the middle of these extremes; they are the kind of people who are generally thoughtful and appreciative in both the giving and receiving of gifts. What kind of gift giver/getter are you? What type of getter is your giftee? The time, money, and effort you spend on a gift might be affected by how you think the gift will be received. A Generous Gift Giver will likely be more conscientious choosing a gift for a Genial Gift Getter because she knows he will genuinely appreciate it. A budget-minded Gratuitous Gift Giver might decide on several small, inexpensive gifts for a Greedy Gift Getter, hoping that quantity over quality might possibly impress him.

The Right Stuff: Tips on Matching the Gift to the Event

After determining what type of giftee you're giving to, the next most important thing to consider is matching the gift to the occasion. Individual tastes, culture, etiquette, your relationship to the giftee—a good number of things can affect what makes for a great gift. The following are a few basics to keep in mind.

- This should probably be understood, but be mindful of the reason for the celebration or occasion: baby stuff for baby showers; fun, "they'd never buy it for themselves" stuff for birthdays; romantic and meaningful gifts for anniversaries; etc. Again, this is no-brainer stuff; just keep in mind that the more in-tune your gift is to the event, the more likely it will wow your giftee.

- Avoid giving "personal" or intimate items as gifts, unless you know for sure that it is something that the giftee would enjoy getting, and that it is appropriate. Things such as see-through underwear for your assistant—because you would love to see him or her wearing them—may not be appreciated (unless they are for you, so that he or she can see you with them on…).

- It's best not to give "gag" or joke gifts, or any gift that may be offensive to anyone, unless the occasion—or the giftee—calls for it. In the art of gift giving, it's always better to be safe than stupid.

- If you really don't have a clue as to what your giftee wants or the kind of gift getter you are gifting to, but you sincerely wish to impress them with your selection, then seriously think about what you would choose for yourself. On the other hand, you can go ahead and make a "chicken choice" and grab a suitable gift card, or something else generic but nice.

- If you do select something "safe" for your gift, at least enclose it in something cool to make it a little more special, like a restaurant gift card wrapped in a Chinese takeout box filled with fun fortunes you've collected (or whole cookies!).

The Right Price: Tips for Gifting on a Budget

Now more than ever, budget can have a huge impact on how we choose gifts. For most people, the ideal gift to give usually has a perceived value equal to or greater than its actual monetary value (which is great when you got a good deal, unless you want people to know you spent less than they thought). Nevertheless, before you spend big or choose to go cheap, keep these tips in mind.

- Match the value of the gift to the occasion, the reason, and the person, as well as the type of giftee you are giving the gift to. You don't want to go crazy on a "just because" gift for a neighbor if it means you won't have the funds to put together an equally impressive anniversary gift for your best friend later on.

- Likewise, if you have to buy for a Genial Gift Getter and a Grumbling Gift Getter at the same time, consider who's more worth pulling out all the stops for (the Genial, who might be happy with something small anyway, or the Grumbling, who would probably find fault with an original Picasso: "Why is it so blue? I hate that color!").

- If your budget—and income—fluctuates, be careful of giving lavish gifts regardless of who they are for and for what occasion when your money is good, especially if those who will be getting gifts when your wallet has dried up will be stiffed. This also applies to acknowledging some friends or family with a generous gift in front of others who will not be so lucky on a similar occasion later on. Better to be frugal and fair than to be overindulgent and inconsistent.

● Keep in mind your personal calendar of gift-giving events as well as your budget allowances for each occasion and particular gift getters. If you plan on giving a birthday gift to every relative, friend, and co-worker, those gifts alone may necessitate a personal loan (if you can get one). Oftentimes, your "gift" could be a phone call, personalized card, or a heartfelt note, but you need to be as realistic and reasonable as possible. (Hint: Regifting could come in really handy here...)

● Don't go overboard for employers, teachers, and other people you want to impress, including rich, distant relatives. "Less is more, and much less is best." It is better to under-gift and include a personal note of appreciation, congratulations, or whatever is appropriate for the occasion, than to over-gift and be perceived as a suck-up.

● If your friends want to "go in" on a gift, the value and quality of the gift should reflect the appropriate number of people participating. Each person should pony up for the part of the gift he or she "gives." And don't let yourself be pressured to let freeloading friends simply sign the card of a prepaid gift—a twenty-dollar gift card as a wedding gift "given" by five people isn't going to impress even a Genial Gift Getter.

To Gift or to Regift? That Is the Question

The answer to this question is quite simple: you can either spend your hard-earned money on some brand-new, just-bought item and hope that it is somewhat suitable and appreciated, or you can spend little to no money on something that may still be "new," just not newly purchased, that will still be totally fitting and appropriate. Finding a good gift in line with what type of giftee you're giving to, the occasion, and your budget can be solved by either shopping for a "virgin" gift (not to be confused with a gift for a virgin) or putting together a gracious regift. Here are a few pros and cons to going either way.

Benefits of giving a virgin gift

- You won't feel guilty or cheap (if you still have hang-ups about regifting)

- Most likely you will have many more options for finding the "right" gift

- It will probably be easier for the giftee to return it, exchange it, or possibly even regift it if they want

- There really are no other gains to giving a virgin gift

Disadvantages of giving a virgin gift

- You will likely spend much more money than on a regift

- You will likely spend much more time trying to find the "right" gift

- "Virgin" status does not guarantee the gift will be liked any more than not

- Since less thought and creativity are involved, the gift is more likely to be generic and impersonal

- It's likely something that they already have

- Someone else may also be giving them the same thing

- You will possibly be adding unnecessary gift waste to our environment

Benefits of giving a regift

- It will cost you next to nothing

- It will lighten your load of "regiftables" or clear out some clutter

- The gift is guaranteed to be "custom" and totally personalized for the person who might really want it

- You won't have to worry about someone else giving them the same thing

- You won't have to waste precious time and gas or find a place to park

- You are recycling an otherwise wasted gift, and all the trimmings

Disadvantages of giving a regift

- It may be considered tactless if known

- You may need to spend extra time embellishing it

- You may not have the "right" gift available in your stash

- There really are no other drawbacks to regifting!

"There is no such thing as a bad regift, only bad regifters."

~regifting proverb

What Is Regifting?
Eliminating Regifting's Bad Rap (Once and for All)

2

Really, the positives and negatives of choosing between a virgin gift or a regift even out in some areas but clearly fall in favor of regifts in others. In my opinion, the biggest disadvantage a regift faces is prejudice. But regifting hasn't always had such a bad reputation. Here's what happened.

Historically, people have been regifting since the beginning of time, and it was accepted in all cultures. A gift was a gift was a gift. Or so everyone thought.

But somehow, as people became more prosperous and shopping malls sprang up, the generous and globally recognized act of regifting became totally taboo. People went around saying ridiculous things, like "Don't look at a regift as if it's been in a horse's mouth." (For some reason this later became "Don't look a gift horse in the mouth," which doesn't make any sense either.)

It was not uncommon to hear scornful clichés like

"Beware of Greeks bearing regifts,"

"Far be regifting it from me,"

"Easy come, easy regift,"

"An apple a day keeps the regift away," and

"Forgive them for regifting—they know not what they do."

Even the almighty Aretha had something cynical to say about it when she recorded "R-E-G-I-F-T-T, regifting isn't meant to be…" (Hey, she was a singer, not a speller.)

So it is really no wonder that the once-popular practice of regifting eventually came to be regarded as pitiful and in poor taste, and was ultimately completely rejected by anyone giving a gift. Mothers began to say of regifts, "It's the thought that counts"—the ultimate blow any gift giver can receive. Regifting became the "dirty little secret" of gift giving, finally relegated only to fruitcakes and guest towels, and reserved for relatives and relationships gone awry.

But now, all of that is about to change.

The goal, of course, is to evoke a major awakening in all of us and, finally, to help foster

A **regifting revival,**

and **the grand redemption**

and (re-)creation of **Gracious Regifting!**

Why a Regifting Revival?

In these days of recycling, reselling, and recession, there needs to be a resurgence of regifting. This can only be good for mankind, the environment, and gift giving in general.

Knowing and understanding how to *properly* regift does not come naturally to most people. To learn how to regift *graciously* takes practice and a little ingenuity (and maybe a little bit of nerve at times—ask anyone in my family!).

The rest of this guide completely covers everything you ever wanted to know, whether you knew you needed to know it or not (and who would you ask, anyway?), about the secrets of successful and *gracious* regifting. In other words, there is definitely a distinct difference between the two. Gracious regifting is regifting of the highest caliber. It's reusing your gifts—to give as gifts—in ways you may have never thought of. Up until now, that is.

Gracious Regifting: A New Twist on an Old Trend

Nowadays, regifting can be so much more than just rewrapping (or not) an unwanted gift you have received and simply passing it on to someone else. Regifting can suit different occasions, different purposes, and different people, for different reasons. There are specific methods of proper, or "gracious," regifting according to various types of regiftable items. And, of course, everything depends on what type of regifter you are, which we'll discuss later on.

So what is the real difference between regular regifting and regifting a gift graciously? Who does it, and why?

First, let us take a look at the traditional definitions of *regifting*.

Re- *prefix* **1** back **2** again; anew

gift *n.* **1** something given; present **2** the act of giving
vt. **1** to present a gift to **2** to present as a gift

regift *n.* a gift that was previously gotten by the giver, but given again to someone else
vt. to give a gift that you had been given before;
(**regifts)** *n.* or *vt.* (**regifting**) *vt.* giving gifts already gotten
(**regifted**) *vt.* a gift given already gotten by the giver

And then let's look at the word *gracious*.

> **gracious** *adj.* 1 having or showing kindness, courtesy, charm, etc. 2 compassionate 3 polite to supposed inferiors, showing fortune 4 marked by luxury, ease, etc. 5 merciful, tender, loving, kind 6 characterized by good taste, comfort 7 benign, friendly, favorable 8 pleasantly condescending 9 using genius, flare, finesse, creativity, cleverness, etc., when regifting.

So in defining *gracious regifting*, we speak of the subtle art of reusing gifts that you have previously received by giving them to someone else in such a genuine, creative, and clever manner that they are still considered to be friendly, tasteful, and favorable by almost any gift getter.

The term *gracious regifting* will unquestionably become the ultimate way to give someone else a gift that you have previously gotten, admirably and excellently.

Gracious Regifting Fundamental #1

Gracious regifting is the subtle art of reusing gifts that you have previously received by giving them as gifts to someone else in such a genuine, creative, and clever manner that they are still considered to be friendly, tasteful, and favorable.

We intend to break it down for you so you can recognize the many varieties among regiftable gifts and master the differences between giving a regift that is terrific—and one that is extremely tacky!

Why YOU Should Regift

Okay, so maybe you buy that there are good ways and bad ways to regift, and that gracious regifting sounds like it could be a cool idea. But maybe you're still befuddled on how to spot a regiftable gift or when a regifted item would be appropriate to give. Well, naturally not all gifts should be regifted, nor would you realistically want to regift everything you get (except maybe the stuff from some of your relatives). However, there are definitely times when you receive a gift that you cannot (or will not) use, despite the honorable (?) intentions of the gift giver. Since you know it would be rude to refuse a gift that someone has given you, for any reason whatsoever, you might think you are stuck with it forever. However, a Gracious Regifter can recognize the regifting potential many of these gifts may possess.

Some examples of times when a gift you get screams "REGIFT!" (or maybe just whispers it a little…) are listed here.

Note: If a gift you got really does scream, or make any unnecessary noises, we suggest you give it back to the giver immediately. Regrettably, there is no good way to graciously regift living, or screaming, things. Don't say we didn't warn you.

Situations When a Received Gift is Justifiably Regiftable

1. You sincerely appreciate the gift (and the giver), but at this time, you do not have a need or a place for it. You will, however, keep it until the right opportunity comes along (and until then, store it with your other regiftable stock).

2. You sincerely appreciate the gift, but you really do already have one of whatever it is, and you don't wish to hurt the gift giver's feelings by returning or exchanging it.

3. The received gift is perfect—perfectly stupid! On the other hand, perhaps it would be perfect for a different person. (What were they *thinking*?)

4. The received gift is something not needed, not liked, not wanted, or not even close to being something useful! (What *were* they thinking?)

5. The received gift is all wrong—wrong size, wrong color, wrong assumption it would be appreciated. Why would someone bother to ask you what you wanted if they are not going to give it to you anyway? (*What* were they thinking?)

6. The received gift is already an obvious regift. (They did not read this book, apparently—or else it is probably from a relative!)

So now you suddenly have a new pile of unused and unwanted gifts that you recognize as having regift potential. But when is it appropriate to regift a gift you've received? The answer to that is, "Just about any gift-giving occasion!" but I'll be a little more specific.

According to experts in the field (and yes, there actually is a regifting field), people regift for a variety of reasons.

10 Reasons When a Regift is a Given:

1. You are invited to a party where a regift is actually requested. (This can really happen!)

2. You win a "great prize" from PTA Bingo Night (or a church raffle or your company picnic—which probably has the company logo on it) that is really not that great. Well, at least not to you…

3. You honestly already have the perfect gift for the recipient in your regift stash, so there is no reason to buy something else. (This can really happen too—lucky you!)

4. You receive a gift from someone for whom you did not get a gift, and now you need to improvise.

5. There is no time (or reason) to shop for a "real" gift, and you have several items "in stock" for just such occasions…

6. You are too broke (or too cheap) to spring for a gift, and no one will let you just sign your name to their card.

7. You are simply too lazy to get up, get out, and go get a good gift. Besides, you don't really know them that well…

8. Truth be told, you simply cannot stand the recipient and couldn't care less whether or not the gift will be appreciated.

> **Paybacks!** If the gift getter is someone you are sure has already regifted to you, and if you really wanted to be an *Un*Gracious Regifter, you could regift *back to* him or her the regift that was *from* them in the first place. What fun!

9. You receive a really silly, bizarre, or lame gift, but it's one that could really be funny to give to someone else who shares your sense of humor.

10. Sometimes, you just want to regift something you already got "just because," and it should not matter what the reason is!

But the very best reason to consider regifting as an option when giving gifts is simple: Why not? Should people really care where a gift came from if the gift is tasteful, appropriate, and a definite token of your affection?

Of course not!

Regifters Are Secretly Living Among Us

You know them. They might live by you, work with you, be related to you. They are everywhere, and almost any gift that they give could be a regift. Their mantra is "A regift is better than no gift," and it can apply to practically anyone. Nevertheless, you will soon learn that is not necessarily a bad thing.

These are the people around you who are likely already regifting.

Your mother: Okay, and your grandmother, brother, cousin—*all* of your relatives have probably already regifted, whether you know it or not!

Your co-worker: Especially if you are the boss, or if no one likes you—and watch for items with the company logo…

Your teacher: Can you really blame them? What else are they supposed to do with thirty-six scented candles or a box full of bath & body trios, coffee mugs, and items with apples on them? Besides, how many adorable desk sets can one desk actually accommodate?

The new bride: This one is a no-brainer. Besides the multiple sets of glassware you get, you only have storage space for one of each kind of kitchen gadget or appliance.

Your neighbor: Some regifts could be old housewarming gifts from other neighbors…so if they have lived there a while, it's probably a regift. And if you live in a transient neighborhood, you will then have the perfect "Welcome, new neighbor!" gift to turn around and give!

🎁 **That person you don't know very well but who has to give you a gift for whatever reason:** Well, what else would you expect?

🎁 **That person you don't like very much, and the feeling is mutual, but who is still somehow obligated to get you something:** This should not surprise you since you would do the same thing, right?

🎁 **Future You:** C'mon, now! You got this book, didn't you? That does not make you a bad person, and besides, it's really not so wrong, we promise!

What's Your Regifting Baseline?

Has your view of regifting been reformed yet? Not only have you learned that there are probably tons of people around you already doing it but that there are actually some very good reasons to regift, and that you can learn to do it really well! But before you begin to use this guide, you first need to find out what kind of a regifter you already are, and how much more you need to know about gracious regifting. Rate your "regifterness" and test your regifting guile with this comprehensive quiz.

◉ **Question #1:** Have you ever been given a gift that you suspected was a regift?

   A. No, I don't think so. But if I did, the person must have read this book!

   B. Probably, since I have gotten many lame gifts and I usually stick them in a donation bag.

   C. Yes, I have because it was so obvious! Please—a box of stationery that states "Part of Set—Not Intended To Be Sold Separately"…?

   D. I am pretty sure I have, especially from people that recently got married or had a big birthday party (to which I was not invited). I do not remember ever asking for a fondue set…

   E. Maybe I did, but if it was something that I wanted, I didn't care. And if it wasn't, then I probably went ahead and regifted it myself!

◉ **Question #2:** If you have ever received a regift, what was it about the gift that made you so suspicious (assuming you were not told)?

   A. That's easy—it's the exact same thing I gave to them last year!

   B. The tag "Merry Christmas, Love, Aunt Joan," along with the gift receipt from 1999 was still inside the jewelry box.

C. Probably when I noticed that their company logo was imprinted on the bottom of the travel clock. Besides, I never asked for a travel clock, nor would I ever, and I would never need one since I never travel.

D. Because any time you get a makeup bag with a lipstick, blush, and eye shadow in colors not found in nature already tucked inside of it (and not sealed in plastic), you know it was a freebie!

E. Only that it was probably the lamest gift I ever got, and there is no way that someone actually saw this somewhere and said, "I know so-and-so would LOVE THIS!"

⦿ **Question #3:** Have you ever given someone a gift, for any reason, that was previously given to you?

A. Are you kidding? I could never be that tacky!

B. No, I never have, but I think I would if I needed to.

C. Well, yes, I did, but it should not count if I actually already had one of whatever it was.

D. Of course! What am I supposed to do with all of the "gifts" that I have accumulated (from my relatives…)?

E. Yes, but I prefer to think of it as passing on a great gift I couldn't use or didn't want, to someone who could or did, so I'm doing the most thoughtful, economical, and environmentally preferred option of all.

◉ **Question #4:** If you have ever actually regifted something (or whatever you feel comfortable in calling it), you

A. Regifted it exactly as it was given to you, without any alterations or repackaging.

B. Stuck some new stickers over the original "To/From" sticker that you could not scrape off or write over successfully.

C. Put the gift as is into a Neiman Marcus gift bag and hoped they would be impressed (or clueless).

D. Frantically washed and rewrapped the set of designer shot glasses you got a couple of years ago but never used, hoping the regiftee wasn't the one who gave them to you, as you were short on time and funds.

E. Took out a couple of things that you wanted from the "Sinfully Sensuous Scents" gift basket you got, added a scented candle and a little massage animal (from a previous gift), carefully reattached the shrink-wrap, and tied it up with a ribbon before you guiltlessly regifted it to someone else.

◉ **Question #5:** If you gave someone a regift, and he or she told you they totally "LOVED IT!" you would:

A. Feel guilty, 'fess up, and attempt to try and somehow explain why you gave them a regift in the first place.

B. Smile shyly, say nothing, and shrug off their appreciation while pointing out the other great gifts they got.

C. Keep quiet about it and accept their gratitude for your great gift idea.

D. Make a joke about it and turn it into an educational forum about the exciting and veritable revival of regifting, and hope you don't get it back one day. (You may also want to include a copy of this book…)

E. Smile knowingly as if you *knew you had found* them the perfect gift, and be super pleased with yourself for doing such a darned good job of graciously regifting!

◉ **Question #6:** If you gave someone a regift with the best of intentions (meaning you really thought it was the right gift for the recipient), but you could tell that they *hated* it, whether or not they suspected it was a regift, you would

A. Apologize profusely, actually admit it was a regift, and sheepishly take it back, promising to get them a "real gift."

B. Apologize profusely and try to explain why you seriously thought they would appreciate it—but *do not* tell them it was a regift.

C. Not give a darn at all since at least you didn't have to waste wads of cash on this ingrate that you didn't even like very much anyway (especially now).

D. Not apologize. Just pretend that you predicted that they might not realize your reason for thinking of that particular present, and then proceed to tell a great story as to why you purposely picked it for them (while not referring to its regift status).

E. Apologize profusely but sincerely (and *only* for your lack of fore-sight and sensitivity), and then strongly suggest that *they* regift it to someone else instead (perhaps with a copy of this book!).

◉ **Question #7:** Do you believe that regifting is an acceptable gift-giving alternative, but unfortunately, due to the rampant corruption and carelessness of so many clueless regifters, regifting has been misjudged, misinterpreted, and misunderstood?

A. No way! I would be so totally insulted if I actually got a regift, and I would certainly never be so incredibly crass as to give one! I think that "regiftable" items are what keep thrift shops in business

B. Well…Maybe I might do it, but I would never admit it. I still think it is kind of tacky (except maybe to your relatives).

C. I have secretly been doing it all along, so maybe now it will not continue to be considered such an inconsiderate and ignorant idea.

D. Yes! I totally agree! However, regifting should almost always be accompanied by a great story if you admit to it—unless you are truly trying to pass it off as "thoughtful, new, and personal."

E. *Yes!* And so I intend to begin changing this misconception immediately by purchasing multiple copies of this book and giving them along with my carefully crafted and impressive regifts! I want to be a Gracious Regifter and start campaigning right now for the good of all gift givers!

◉ **Question #8:** Give yourself a point for each reason you would consider regifting:

A. At this time, I still would *not* consider regifting, unless I was truly desperate. (**Subtract a point** for this answer…)

B. If I didn't know the person and/or didn't really care

C. If I had whatever the giftee wanted and specifically asked for

D. If I received a lot of gifts that I didn't want or couldn't use but maybe someone else could

E. Because I can.

⊙ **Question #9:** Give yourself a point for each of the following items you would consider regifting.

    A. Personalized or monogrammed items

    B. Promotional items, or "freebies"

    C. Food items, jewelry, or books

    D. Gifts from relatives

    E. Any item you would have to invent a use for

⊙ **Question #10:** Give yourself a point for each of the following people you would consider regifting to.

    A. Your boss

    B. Your neighbor

    C. The bride and groom

    D. Your best friend

    E. Your mother (or other family member, including your spouse)

For your answers to questions 1–7, give yourself:

1 point for each A

2 points for each B

3 points for each C
4 points for each D
5 points for each E

Add any additional points from questions 8–10, and now tally up your total score. (If you answered anything but "E" to most of the quiz questions, you still have much to learn anyway, no matter what your score. So keep reading!)

Your score will help you determine what type of regifter you are at the present time. (Please excuse the pun.)

If you scored **less than 25** points, you currently reign as a **Below Average, or non-**regifter. A score of **26–36** points means right now you meet the terms of an **Average** regifter. Scoring **37–50** points on this quiz officially qualifies you as an **Above Average** regifter. (If you scored **45+** points on the "regifter scale," you already meet the rigorous demands of a **Regifting Guru**! I bow to you, and beg you to teach some classes…!

Next, we'll take a closer look at what your rating means and how it relates to the different types of regifters and their regifting styles.

> NOTE: These "regifter qualities" are specific to regifting and are not intended to classify or judge the individual character traits, or the actual personality of the regifter, even though they may be similar.

Different Sorts of Regifters

Regifters can be sorted into three general classifications.

BELOW AVERAGE: It's obvious that the Non-Regifters and Regifting Goobers make this grade, but sad to say, even a Regular Regifter falls here. They are most likely indiscriminate regifters as well—the aimless sorts who don't really care if they regift or not, as long as their gift-giving obligation is fulfilled in the most convenient (and cheapest) way. Most of them probably only regift in an emergency in the first place. They are also usually clueless about an appropriate gift selection when it comes to gift giving in general, let alone figuring out the most fitting regift. They will normally choose whatever regiftable they find handy, one that requires the least amount of effort to regift. Sometimes their technique is limited to changing the "to" to "from" on the gift tag. Of these regifter types, neither recognizes, nor even pays mind to any other aspect of the gift-giving process. If they need a gift, they find a gift to give, one way or another, no matter what or from where. However, for a Regular Regifter, there is a plus to their random regifting ways. They generally do possess a bit of pride and most likely will only regift something brand-new and unopened. Fortunately for you, though, if you are simply ignorant about the mode of regifting, and have only not yet been introduced to the many wonderful ways of reusing your gifts wisely and graciously, then pay close attention. You will be amazed at how quickly you can soon claim a more acceptable regifter status.

AVERAGE: Although you can't really accuse Good Regifters of serious flaws in their regifting abilities, their style is more laid back and elementary—with not too much enhancement. They are quite comfortable with the regifting concept but are generally not willing to go the extra mile when it comes to regifting graciously. However, if they are simply inexperienced and only lacking in some skills and expertise, then they can refine and improve their regifting style fairly easily. Even if they are not all that interested in bettering their regifting ability, the average regifter will not adversely affect the reputation of regifting unless they choose to do so by regularly doing stupid stuff.

ABOVE AVERAGE: Regifters in this group are those who have no problem with the regifting concept and, in fact, actually take pride in their regifterness. Most will usually regift whenever possible, though some might still regift only under certain circumstances. They include your Great and Gracious Regifters, whose skillful techniques will vary from gift to gift, gift getter to gift getter. All are conscientious and clever in their regifting manners. (Getting to an even higher level—the fabled Regifting Guru status—takes fortitude, experience, and technique perfection in giving all types of regifts. Nevertheless, those willing to persevere and put forth the effort will eventually reach their lofty regifter goals.)

On the Road to Gracious Regifting

If you are reading this book, you probably fall somewhere in the average or below-average regifter range, and you have decided that you need a little guidance and upgrading on your regifting techniques (or someone you know is giving you a big hint). On the other hand, perhaps the idea of regifting is totally foreign to you, but you're curious to see what all the fuss is about.

Well, then, good for you! Admitting that you are a non-regifter, a rotten regifter, or a regifting goof is the first step to regift rehabilitation and total recovery. And we can help.

Now is the time to embrace your regifting know-how (or lack thereof) and shamelessly reveal it to the world (or at least to your friends and family). If we are truly going to make gracious regifting seriously be considered the number-one way to recycle unwanted and unnecessary gifts, then global awareness is the key. Almost everybody has regifted something to someone at some time or another, either by choice or by chance. But was the regift really stupid—or absolutely stellar? Was it considered cheap and cheesy or fabulous (and mostly free!)? Did you feel clever and crafty or downright despicable doing it?

Practically everyone has a favorite personal "regifting story," either as the regift giver or the regift getter. Go ahead—ask someone. No matter whom you talk to, undoubtedly "it has happened to them."

When you finish this book, you will no longer be reluctant to regift. Soon you will be able to regift without any guilt or shame whatsoever. You finally will have the tools, the inclination, and the good taste to become a really great Gracious Regifter.

Gracious Regifting Fundamental #2

Almost any gift received can be regifted, but not all gifts can be regifted in just any way!

You too can become a Regifting Guru!

Just please always remember the most pertinent rule for regifting: Almost *any* gift received can be regifted, but not all gifts can be regifted in just *any* way! If you are going to regift, you need to do it right! A Gracious Regifter has standards.

Remember,

a **Gracious Regifter** regifts with cleverness and class,

a **Great Regifter** regifts with flair and a little flash,

a **Good Regifter** does so ideally with some ingenuity and imagination,

while a **Regular Regifter's** gifts rarely cause a sensation,

and a **Regifting Goober** (and you know who they are) just make regifting seem awkward and inappropriate for all.

"If at first you don't like your gift, try, try to regift it."

~regifting proverb

3
The Master List of Regiftables

The "GAG" experts have identified more than twenty types of items that typically tend to be regifted more often than others. You probably have received a few of them yourself. If you should ever plan to *give* one of these gifts to someone else, you will now be able to guess just what might happen to it (and hopefully you won't get it back!). You will also get some ideas for some of the savviest methods in which to graciously regift these gifts, should you actually get one and not want it or need it.

With that matter in mind, a regift rating system has been added to help you easily determine the level of difficulty you could potentially face in order to properly and graciously regift each particular type of regiftable item. Some regift types are simpler than others, in terms of creativity, and will require less effort to present in an appropriate and satisfactory way.

🎁 Super simple

You could possibly get away with regifting these items without much "enhancement"—or perhaps only some simple repackaging is necessary.

🎁 🎁 Fairly easy

These items are not *too* unusual, so with a little repackaging, embellishments, and/or additions, you will be good to go in order to graciously regift it.

🎁 🎁 🎁 A tad tricky

These items may take a little more imagination and inventiveness to successfully graciously regift them; however, if you are experienced, you can probably pull it off.

🎁 🎁 🎁 🎁 Difficult

These are the types of gifts people get that can sit around for years before an occasion arises where they could actually become an ideal gift for someone else. The catch is, since they have been around for quite some time because of the sheer absurdity of the gift or because determining who would actually want the gift is head scratching, it's up to a master Gracious Regifter to make it work. These items are certainly not for the timid, or novice, regifter;

however, practice really does make perfect. You still will have to consider the regift getter…

Regifting Gurus only!

These gifts are the epitome of the highest level of gracious regifting achievement. Your regifting reputation is on the line here. Unless you have proved your regifting prowess on numerous occasions, and your talents are literally legendary (like mine), then you may as well "fuggedaboudit"! Do not even attempt to graciously regift these gift types unless you are confident in your creativity and craftiness.

Many of these gift types could certainly fall into more than one category. While some of the regifting methods may be similar, each technique does, in fact, have some subtle differences. It is up to you to decide on the one style most suitable, depending on the circumstances in which you received the gift and to whom you are graciously regifting it.

Types of Gifts that Typically Tend to Get Regifted

#1 The Alien

This is a gift that you have received and yet have absolutely no idea what it is. Or what it's for! Most likely, it was sent through the mail (probably from a relative), so you cannot get an immediate explanation. Even if you do finally figure out what it is, it may still be difficult to understand just

how someone actually put thought into giving this gift to you—especially a relative (or perhaps that alone is explanation enough).

It is only natural to want to regift the **Alien** to someone else. If you did indeed receive it by mail from out of state, then it's a safe bet that you can graciously regift it—as is, if you know what it is—to just about anyone without the guilt or the giver ever guessing. (However, this can be a problem if they pay you a surprise visit and worriedly wonder aloud about the whereabouts of the expensive, "one of a kind" wall hanging they sent you from the Sichuan region of Southwest China. That one you thought was a tablecloth that you graciously regifted to someone who actually appreciated the efforts of pandas that can paint...)

Tips for Gracious Regifting

If you do decide to regift an **Alien**—and you may not have a choice—you might want to hang on to it for a while, just in case. Otherwise, you can just make up what it is and what it could be used for, or say it reminded you of them. It's best if you can send it instead of giving it in person. You can always act as if you "accidentally sent the wrong gift" depending on their reaction.

Best regifted to

- someone who has a great sense of humor,

- someone who you don't see very often,

- someone you don't know very well but to whom you have to give a gift,

- someone you don't like very much but to whom you have to give a gift,

- a relative you don't see very often, you don't know very well or like very much but to whom you have to give a gift.

Regifting Scenario

You received from your sister what you thought was a giant potato scrubber, so you regifted it as a giant potato scrubber, which would have been okay, except that you found out it was actually a corn and callous remover. (But it sure makes a great potato scrubber!)

#2 The ASOTI ("As Seen On TV" item)

It used to be that you could only buy **ASOTIs** actually from TV commercials or infomercials. Now you can purchase many of them in various other places, including actual retail stores bearing the name. Certainly, there are loads of legitimate and reputable products available that are marketed with that particular tagline. Over the last decade, a good number of **ASOTI**s have made their way into most modern homes. Some people are completely confident in the quality of any item seen and advertised on TV, and then there are others who question the caliber of any **ASOTI** affiliation whatsoever, if only on principle. If you consider yourself one of the latter, and you are given an **ASOTI** that you feel you could not or would not use under any circumstance, then, of course, you would probably deem it as regiftable.

Tips for Gracious Regifting

Graciously regifting an **ASOTI** is quite simple and similar to the ideas for any of the low-maintenance regiftables, unless of course it also falls under the more challenging types. Since some stuff looks a lot better on TV (especially late at night), these items will be when your gracious regifting prowess will be put to the test, unless you don't wish to be so clever or discreet. You can at least repackage it in an appropriate manner or regift it as a joke or as a **Perpetual Present**, especially if you have no idea whether or not your giftee would even appreciate a handy "bra ball" or a "guaranteed enhancement tool." If you genuinely believe that your giftee would be pleased and appreciative of this particular item, then it won't really matter whether you regift it, graciously or not. Your gift would still be regarded favorably!

"But wait, there's more…"

Best regifted to

- just about anybody, if it's something you know they would actually like and/or if they asked for it.

Regifting Scenario:

You received a leather "everything bag" that didn't quite live up to its claim, but your neighbor was just going on about how handy one would be...

#3 The BIB (Bought In Bulk)

For all you bargain hunters and shrewd shoppers, this is probably one of your favorite kinds of gifts to give, but not necessarily one to get. Like a **Fab Find** (discussed later), it is usually a great find, but unlike a **Fab Find**, it is always actually purchased. You will know your gift is a **BIB** if what you got is like what everyone else got also. This happens a lot in classrooms and large families. All of the girls get one gift, and all of the guys get something else.

This category includes multiples of catalog items and things that you bought more than one of (not necessarily for yourself) because it was such a dynamic deal you could hardly pass it up. Clearance sales, closeouts, lot sales, bargain bins, "going out of business" items, and purchasing "lots of things you don't need but could use them for gifts," using in-store discounts and coupons all count as **BIBs**. Buying a bunch of souvenirs from somewhere (as with the **Souvenir**) could count here, too.

Regift Exception #1

If something has been sitting in storage over a period of time with no particular gift getter in mind, or if any of the products were purchased with the intention of giving them as gifts at some point, then it becomes a "generic regift" and is graciously regifted accordingly.

You know you have done this! How could you resist the "everything drastically reduced!" sale of ornamental glass insect figurines and the "lowest price of the season" personalized note cards (with names of no one you even know) that they were practically giving away? Just think, now that you have stocked up on this stuff, some day when you actually need a gift for an "Anjelluh," or "Merrianne," you will be all set, and maybe she would love a crystal cockchafer, too! (Seriously, look it up.)

Most gifters of **BIBs** probably do not consider themselves regifters—just frugal—because you cannot technically regift something that you never actually received as a gift, graciously or not, but **BIBs** represent Regift Exception #1.

Tips for Gracious Regifting

If you are a big believer of buying in bulk, and do so regularly, then you already know that in 99 percent of any of *your* regular gift-giving occasions, you simply grab a gift from your previously purchased gift stock instead of actually giving a gift that was handpicked and purchased especially for your gift getter. (Even though, sometimes, it may still prove to be a most thoughtful and perfect gift for that person.) To (hopefully) get around this potential problem, you could make a **BIB** your signature gift, which means that you will always give a particular gift for a particular occasion.

Best regifted to

- teachers,
- neighbors,

- co-workers,

- gift getters who wouldn't be insulted to get a gift that you got
  for everyone.

Regifting Scenario

At an annual buying blitz from an outlet mall, you purchase mega sets of tea towels in various colors. For all of your friends' birthdays every year you give them each a set in their favorite color, either as all or part of their gift. It's a "tradition."

#4 The Collectible

Have you ever noticed that when you are partial to a particular hobby, sport, team, car, animal, insect, or other personal obsession, you receive many gifts pertaining to it? In reality, you can only use so many decks of Harley-Davidson playing cards, golf club covers that look like past presidents, or kitchen doohickeys adorned with chickens. In some cases, you may not even realize that you have amassed quite a "collection" of a particular type of trinket until you realize that you have received a great many of them from the same gift giver (who is probably a relative).

That is why this category can also apply to people (such as parents) who are trying to unload their own accumulation of clutter, usually under the facade of things being "family heirlooms," or stuff they were "saving for you." Go figure.

So, if your assortment of gewgaw is getting out of control, then regifting is the obvious answer.

Tips for Gracious Regifting

It is important to regift this lot only to others that share the passion and same interests as you do. If you are not exactly sure, it is better to hang on to these regiftables for a future occasion and giftee. It could be tough to figure out a distinctive way to graciously regift duplicates of your vintage doily collection. And, of course, you wouldn't want to regift a Redskins mug to a Dallas fan (or would you?). If it's actually an item your giftee collects, or would like, then you don't really have to do anything else to the regift. If it's a "fringe" collectible, meaning your giftee doesn't *officially* collect the item, if at all, you could always regift it as the start of a collection, perhaps with one or more from your own collection.

Best regifted to

- relatives,

- friends,

- anyone who likes, or currently collects, the specific items, or you want them to.

Regifting Scenario:

You have acquired a ridiculous amount of thimbles, which you really did collect about thirty-five years ago…and some people think that you still do. Wouldn't you like to get your niece set up with a fine thimble collection? (You could call them "heirlooms"…)

#5 The Perpetual Present

This is truly the gift that keeps on giving. It gets graciously regifted between friends and families forever and ever, usually annually (e.g., Christmas or birthdays). Sometimes these gifts may be symbolic, goofy gag items, or just silly, stupid stuff. (Even greeting cards can be repeatedly regifted!) It is usually a lot of fun, and normally everyone knows it is a regift (or at least they are supposed to). Sometimes the gift may previously have been an actual gift or a regift, like a **Chronic Regift** or a **TUI** that became a joke. The idea is that you purposely regift it to someone who regifts it again to someone else, and so on. Alternatively, you could pass it back and forth between yourself and just one other person. (About fifteen years ago, my mother gave my husband a bottle of "Navy" cologne because he was in the Navy, of course. He regifted it to my brother, also in the Navy, and they have been regifting it back and forth ever since.) Nevertheless, there is almost always a good story behind the gift, which is part of the fun. If there isn't a story, just make one up! You can contrive a convincing explanation for just about everything, right?

Tips for Gracious Regifting

Sometimes it can be extremely entertaining (or even part of the "tradition") if you come up with a creative way to present the **Perpetual Present**.

Seeing how you can best outdo each other with your originality and/or your wild and wacky wit in the "how and where" the gift is given, even who delivers it, can definitely be an intriguing element in this game!

In the event that this **Perpetual Present** is something that you are supposed to purposely pass on to someone where it's not meant as a joke, e.g., a friendship ball, baptismal gown, or a traveling pair of pants, there are usually specific instructions included as to how you are to regift it. For example, a "Wedding Basket," filled with all kinds of appropriate goodies, could be bestowed from couple to couple in a family or tight social group. The basket is given as a gift to the bride and groom, who keep the basket and then fill it with new stuff to give to the next couple to get married or to celebrate an anniversary, and so on. You can always enhance or embellish this regift, but it's usually not necessary unless that's part of the plan.

Best regifted to

- relatives,

- close friends,

- anyone you think would continue regifting it.

Regifting Scenario:

Take an odd vase that you either received as a gift or purchased long ago but never used and completely embellish it with fake gems for your friend's birthday gift. For the next friend's birthday, the vase gets decorated again, but differently, to regift to that friend, and so on. Decorate it each time in a way that personalizes it for the BD giftee. If she loves cooking, stick some wooden spoons in it and dangle a couple of potholders from the top (she probably already got a tea towel).

#6 The Prize Package 🎁

Yay! You won, you won! Nevertheless, just because you won it does not mean you want it—even though it was kind of cool to collect it! What to do, what to do…? Well, at least one thing you will not have to worry about when receiving the **Prize Package** is hurting a friend's feelings because you don't appreciate their perfect present!

> Note: Your bowling trophy and the esteemed "Hairiest Back" plaque do not apply to this category. There are only three options for those types of award winnings: save 'em, display 'em, or discard 'em. In the case of your "Hairiest Back" plaque, and any other disturbing citations, we suggest you simply destroy 'em…

Normally the **Prize Package** will be something nice, and brand-new, since apparently someone thought it seemed like a good prize. Although, it is possible that it was already a regift by the person who compiled the prizes. But why should it matter? If you won it but don't want it, then you will just graciously regift it to someone who will, right?

Tips for Gracious Regifting

It's easy to regift it if it is truly a good prize, and probably no further enhancement is necessary. You can graciously regift it in several ways, mainly using tips from most of the many methods we cover. However, if it is in anyway odd, silly, stupid, or simply something useless to most of us, it may be more difficult to regift, especially if everyone you know now knows you won it, knows you did not want it, and is wondering which one of them is eventually going to get it as a regift! Then it really will depend on whom you are planning to graciously regift it to. (You could also regift it as a **Perpetual Present**...)

Best regifted to

- anyone who doesn't know you won it, and you think would like to have it,

- anyone you don't really know well enough, or don't care enough about, to go to a lot of trouble for by regifting graciously.

Regifting Scenario:

You won a three-tiered sterling silver candy dish, which would make a perfect housewarming or bridal shower gift. No enhancement is necessary, but you may want to throw in some Skittles. You could also graciously regift it as a **Remarketer** and place the set of twenty-four miniature "heirloom" holiday ornaments on it that you received last Christmas. (That would also count then as a **Seasonal** regift.)

#7 The 2fer 🎁 🎁

This is a gift you have received that includes two or more items, multiple pieces, or attachments, e.g., a gift basket filled with goodies or a cookie jar that comes with a matching coffee mug.

These are actually great gifts to get because, although you could just regift the entire package as is, depending on the gift getters you plan to regift to, why not share the wealth?

Tips for Gracious Regifting

To properly graciously regift a **2fer**, you split the items between two or more regift recipients, or regiftees, making sure to add to, enhance, embellish, or repackage the items as needed.* Consider the type of gift getters when deciding how to divvy up the gifts.

 * If you want to keep some of the stuff for yourself and regift the rest, then refer to the tips for regifting a **Partial Regift**.

Best regifted to

* anyone you think would appreciate it, depending on the gift.

Regifting Scenario

You received a gift set of ice cream bowls, a scoop, and an assortment of sundae toppings in a cute "igloo." The easiest way to break it up is to repackage the bowls and scooper in a different container, e.g., a one-gallon size or larger ice cream tub (you could even decorate the tub or the scoop…), and shrink-wrap the toppings in with the "igloo" for the second gift.

#8 The BOGO

You know when you purchase something, and it is "buy one, get one free"? Sometimes it's not something you really need two of. (Why don't they just deduct the cost of the extra item from the actual purchase price if you only want one, anyway?) This also includes items that, when purchased, you also get a smaller version of the item, e.g., buy a large "Confederate" candle and receive a smaller candle "for free." (Although sometimes these smaller, "free" items are simply sample sizes that they could not sell anyway.) This gift could also be one, some of, or all of those extra goodies you get when you buy makeup or tools that include additional free items or the add-ons you receive when you make a major purchase, such as a super turbo-charged vacuum cleaner that comes with a free steam iron or a car vacuum. Anything bought from an infomercial that comes with one of those "And, that's not all" additional free gifts or "if you call within the next five minutes, we'll double your order" offers counts here as well. ("You only have to pay a little extra for shipping and handling" usually adds up to more than the cost of the item anyway.) You might as well get your money's worth and regift whatever you can, unless you actually want the add-ons.

BOGOs as regifts do not have to be bogus. If you are a really shrewd (and smart) shopper, you can wipe out almost an entire list of giftees with just a few purchases!

Tips for Gracious Regifting

Depending on the quality of the items, the "GO" gift of the **BOGO** may not be so tough to regift, even without adding anything extra, unless the free items resemble the "uncool" kinds of stuff you sometimes get with **Freebies** or **Promos** (more on those in a bit). If that is the case, and regifting is still your answer, then adding to the regift or repackaging it will probably be a better idea.

Best regifted to

- anyone who wouldn't know (or guess) that their regift didn't cost a dime, or wouldn't care, as long as it was worth it.

Regifting Scenario:

When you purchased the giant-screen TV, it came with a DVD recorder and a portable DVD player. Now, you have two pretty good gifts to graciously regift, with no need for any embellishments; however, unless you give them together, you may want to add to the portable DVD player. For the portable player, you could include a gift card from a movie rental place or a couple of good DVDs, depending on whom you are giving it to.

#9 The Partial Gift 🎁 🎁

This received gift also includes multiple items, as with the **BOGO** or the **2fer**; however, they are in sets of two or more of the same type of item, e.g., picture frames, candles, colognes, and some clothing sets that come with extras, like a sweater and matching scarf. With this regift, you actually like and/or could use at least one of the items in the set, so you keep that part of the gift for yourself.

Tips for Gracious Regifting

In this regift method, you simply keep what you want and graciously regift the rest, or keep it to add to another regift later. Again, you will probably want to add to, embellish, or repackage the regiftable items between one or more regiftees. (It works best if the items are not all being regifted at the same event.)

Best regifted to

- anyone who wouldn't know (or guess) that their regift was actually only part of a gift but would be pleased with whatever the gift was anyway, as long as it was worth it.

Regifting Scenario:

You receive a set of terra cotta planters that included a few garden tools and a funky-looking garden flag. You don't need the planters or the garden tools, but the flag is pretty cool and colorful, so you want to keep that. Then you can either break up the set of pots and the tools and regift them separately or regift them altogether as one gift. To graciously regift it, you could repackage the garden tools inside one of the pots and toss in a couple of seed packets. Then you could graciously regift the other planters separately as a set, adding to it or not (bonus points if you decorate or paint the pots).

#10 The Upscaler 🎁 🎁

You receive a gift that has obviously been purchased from a low-end retail establishment, cheap catalog, online store, or any warehouse-type shop, and it is something you don't really want. However, you can actually improve its perceived quality through regifting.

Tips for Gracious Regifting

A little ingenuity is required here. It's not necessarily the type of gift that is hard to regift, it is that the gift is probably really cheap-looking already. But classy stores sell junk too, so don't let that deter you from attempting to graciously regift this. Repackage it into a better-quality box or bag from a higher-end retailer, particularly if it is embellished with a well-known store brand. Using logoed tissue or wrapping paper is good, too. You can also try adding tags or stickers from fancier establishments in order to more graciously regift it. Or repackage it with something actually from the store you want your giftee to presume the entire gift came from (hopefully they won't try to return or exchange it...). Be sure there are no "Silver Dollar Store" imprints anywhere on the item. If your giftee is very label conscious, then you may be able to distract them from the actual quality of the regift with the pretentious packaging. Maybe.

Best regifted to

- relatives,

- co-workers,

- teachers,

- so-so friends,

- anyone who would appreciate the actual item, or the fact that it "came from" an expensive or place of higher-quality merchandise.

Regifting Scenario

The "Everyman's a Handyman" tool belt you received from "Hank's Hardware & Bait Shop" would be considered a much better regift if you belted it around a genuine, orange "Home Despot" employee apron emblazoned with their logo (maybe even stencil the giftee's name on it, or perhaps include a couple of **Promo or Freebie** items from the store).

#11 The Freebie 🎁 🎁 🎁

These could actually be great gifts, as long as they are from people who work for, work with, or hang around very important people (like media personalities, or VIPs from movie and music stores, etc.) who are able to score *and* give away really cool free stuff, like DVDs, CDs, concert tickets, movie passes, posters—stuff that has some real value. Free gifts that come from the entertainment or travel industries are best, as well as some stuff (like ball caps and T-shirts) that are shot out of cannons, or given out at concerts, ball games, and grand openings. Sometimes gift cards and gift certificates from restaurants and other great places will work, too. (But if the free stuff you're getting is so awesome, unless you just get too much of it, why would you want to regift it?)

On the other hand, there are also numerous UNcool **Freebies** that you might get that you won't want to keep for yourself, things like magnets, chip clips, flying disks, and various product samples. (However, if they have some company logo on them, they are really **Promo** items.)

Tips for Gracious Regifting

Some **Freebies** are indeed valuable and so can make great regifts, like the free stuff you get at trade shows and conventions, and stuff from radio jocks. However, free stuff that comes in the mail or is stuck in the plastic bag your newspaper comes in…you really wouldn't try to regift those things, would you? Seriously, not even to your relatives, okay? Unless you—or they—are homeless, trying to be humorous, or are extremely hard up! Although, if you are truly up to the creative challenge of attempting to graciously regift a **Freebie**, you may want to group several of these **Freebies** into one regift. Perhaps you could save all of the hotel soaps, mini sewing kits, shower caps, shoe-shine cloths, and deodorant samples you have somehow acquired and arrange them in a basket you kept from a **2fer** or a **Partial Gift**. Then you would really have a special gift that you could graciously regift (seriously—just kidding!).

Best regifted to
- friends,

- co-workers,

- some relatives,

- people you don't know very well (if the Freebies are somewhat lame).

Regifting Scenario
Graciously regift the four-pack of front-row tickets to The Dobies you got for being the first in line for their pre-concert photo-op (you misunderstood and thought you were waiting for The Doobies) by including the autographed picture that you received and their newest—and only—CD to your boss's kid, who's a big fan. (And it couldn't hurt your annual review.)

#12 The Souvenir 🎁 🎁 🎁

Yeah, we know. Your parents went to Turtle Beach, and all you got was a lousy T-shirt. Or maybe it was a miniature flip-flop keychain or a shiny shell ashtray. Whatever it was, you probably do not want it. (Unless, of course, you are a collector of souvenir stuff like spoons and shot glasses from all fifty states. We are not judging; we just don't want them around.)

Some **Souvenirs** are quite cool and unique and are keepers, like the ones from museums and zoos. Even some **Souvenirs** purchased in airports may be good. Undoubtedly, however, the ones that you will want to regift are those that are sold in *every* gift shop in *every* tourist town. They are just imprinted with names of different places.

To be fair, as well as thorough, we would have to include in this category—although they could also be included as a **Promo** item—items that are from, or are indicative of, where you live that you purchase to eventually give as gifts. This is especially true if you live in a touristy or historical area, or somewhere that is well known or famous for particular products, like hams or peanuts or authentic sushi sets. If you reside in Toledo, for example, you might want to keep an ample supply of glassware and Tony Packo's pickles on hand or whatever else it is that Toledo is known for (buckeyes?) for use as regifts to out-of-town relatives and friends.*

Regifting Revival!
Jodi Newbern

Tips for Gracious Regifting

Souvenirs can be somewhat tricky to graciously regift, especially if they are labeled with a specific logo or locality that you have never been to. They can easily be included as part of another package, along with embellishments or add-ons. The only **Souvenirs** outstanding enough to go solo as a regift have to be really special, but then those are probably the ones that you want to keep for yourself. On the other hand, you could always plan to vacation in the very same spots where the **Souvenirs** came from. Then you could graciously regift *those* to your friends and family, which would certainly save you a lot of loot!

*Refer to Regift Exception #1. The purchase of several souvenirs purposely to only give as presents (to no one in particular at this time) could also be considered a **BIB**.

Best regifted to (especially if they do not reside in your town)

- friends,

- co-workers,

- relatives.

Regifting Scenario

Just because you have never been on a cruise doesn't mean your gift getter wouldn't want to. Graciously regift the souvenir wind-up cruise ship and beach towel that you received from your cruising cousin, throw in some cheap sunglasses, suntan lotion, miniature beach chair—whatever you have that will complete the regift—with the BD message: "Your ship finally came in—Happy Birthday!"

#13 The Do-Over

This is another name for old, previously gotten but not yet given gifts, or even "gently used" items (that at some point in time may also have been gifts you got long ago) that have been sitting around awhile. These items might also have been purchased at thrift shops, yard sales, antique stores, flea markets, etc. (No matter how much the giver thinks the giftee would love getting it, unless it's brand-spanking new and has never before been given or gotten, it's still a regift!) If you receive a **Do-over** and you did not actually ask for it, you might as well go ahead and graciously regift it.

Tips for Gracious Regifting

You can actually graciously regift that unusual knickknack or the set of marble coasters you never used or that lovely urn you have had for years (make sure it is empty…). You will just need to clean it, wash it, or dust it off, making sure it is not in need of any repairs, and then add to, embellish, or repackage it accordingly. (Better still if it's in its original, unblemished packaging.) This could possibly be a case where you may want to inform the giftee that it is a regift, unless he or she is yet still an anti-regifter, or you do an outstanding job graciously regifting it! (On the other hand, if you have actually been seen using the punch bowl you wrapped up…) See Regift Exception #2.

Best regifted to

- a relative,

- a neighbor,

- a friend,

- a co-worker.

Regifting Scenario

If someone gave you, long ago, a small carry-on travel bag that, when fully opened can hold about two weeks' worth of wardrobe, yet collapses into a bag small enough to practically put in your purse, would you be impressed? Indeed—so I used it. A couple of times, actually. Then I lost track of it through several moves, only to "discover" it once again, but I had already replaced it. But it still looked brand-new, was still in the box it came in, and would be a perfect gift for my frequent-flyer friend. As a bona fide Gracious Regifter, I couldn't just wrap up the box and give it to her, so I added a few things. Inside each of the pockets, I tucked a mini first-aid kit, some little lotions, etc. (So what if they were all regifted **Freebies**?)

#14 The IDer 🎁 🎁 🎁 🎁

Unfortunately, for you, this gift already has your name on it—literally (or your monogram). This was a lovely idea for a "virgin gift," but it is tough to regift.

In another similar gift situation, when you carefully check for previous personalization on the gift you intend to graciously regift, sometimes you will find that your name has been written on the item packaging. Older people do this to remember whom they bought it for in the first place. (If there is someone's name on it other than yours, it is highly likely that it was already a regift!)

Tips for Gracious Regifting

This one is easy—if you're lucky enough to have a giftee with the same name or initials that you can regift it to. Otherwise, if you still want to graciously regift an **IDer**, you will have to camouflage or hide the name or initials if they cannot be easily removed. You can try to cross it off, write over it with a permanent marker, and/or you could cover it with a sticker—making sure that you cannot see what is underneath or that the sticker can't simply be pulled off (your giftee may become suspicious). You can also try to change it to the regift getter's name, but this can be tricky unless you are very, very good. However, if it is permanently personalized and you can neither get it off nor cover it up, you will have to come up with something clever that the letters, if it's a monogram, might stand for, like an acronym. And, of course, an item imprinted with an actual name like "Mildred" is harder to justify than one imprinted with a name like "Dick."

Best regifted to

- anyone, if you can conceal or remove the name,

- anyone who shares the same name or initials,

- anyone who will believe you if you pretend the name or letters are there on purpose and they mean…

Regifting Scenario

I won't name any names…but when one of my aunts purchased an embroidery machine, every article of clothing bought was monogrammed and given as gifts to various family members. Luckily, she wasn't that skilled at first, so a very cool patchwork vest (that unfortunately was too small for me) was able to be graciously regifted successfully by ironing on little patches over the tops of each of the twelve lovely Js embroidered on each square of the vest front. This little enhancement gave the "umbrella vest" a homemade touch, too.

#15 The Promo 🎁 🎁 🎁 🎁

Whenever you get one of those pocket calendars, pens, notepads, refrigerator magnets, key chains, and other useless promotional items from your banker, realtor, insurance guy, etc., what do you do with them? Do you really think that getting something that says, "Compliments of…" is actually meant as a compliment? Unless you really do need it or want it and do not care that it is sporting a company logo, usually these things just get tossed into a drawer. You may risk hurting the gift giver's feelings if you joke about its regiftability, especially if it was really intended as a great gift. Is it possible that the gift was something the giver thought you would like *because* of the logo? (Like say, for instance, you were once a valid investor in Bear Stearns. Wouldn't you want the wallet with the deeply embossed *BS?*) Perhaps the present was actually purchased especially for you using points they received for Employee of the Month.

Tips for Gracious Regifting

Just what the **Promo** item is will determine its gracious regiftability, as well as the name of the person, school, or company printed on it. Unless it is a useful tote bag, you actually own the business, or you are passing out iPods emblazoned with your company's brand, it is usually best to forget about regifting it, especially if it is something with a cheesy photo plastered on the front. However, if you still feel strongly about graciously regifting it, you can always add something to a **Promo** gift, or add the **Promo** to another regift. Perhaps you could put the free bottle you got of Kick Butt BBQ Sauce in with the logoed lunch box you received (FREE! after your tenth lunch), and graciously regift it to someone who really likes to eat Loud Larry's Rockin' Ribs!

Best regifted to

- co-workers (if they don't have access to logoed products),
- relatives (especially if it's a cool company),
- neighbors,
- friends.

Regifting Scenario

The calculator that opens itself up, the keyboard lights up, and then folds itself back up again when finished is a totally cool tool, and since the company brand is on the bottom, maybe no one will notice. You could combine it with the company-branded leather binder for a super-gracious regifting idea. (Perhaps you could really go all out and throw in another **Promo** or **Freebie** pen…)

#16 The Chronic Regift 🎁 🎁 🎁 🎁 🎁

Before you decide on a gift for someone, don't you usually want to give something that you think the gift getter would actually like, or at least something that you might even pick out for yourself? Apparently, that is not the way it works for some people. Usually a **Chronic Regift** is such a "unique" (read *lame*) gift that, although it is possible that it really was picked out just for you personally, normally this type of gift is something that *no one* would really want, and it is almost *always* regifted, or at least stored somewhere for someone later. Sometimes people may hang on to it awhile before regifting it again, so that everyone has perhaps forgotten about it. You might also want to wait to regift it after you have moved, gotten a new job, or are invited to a (relative's) wedding. It is out of your hands—and your house—from there, and hopefully it will stay out!

Tips for Gracious Regifting

There is really very little to do to help this gift become an honored gracious regift. No matter how creatively you improve upon it, it will most likely get regifted again. And again. You may just want to admit defeat, perhaps give a (Re)Gift Receipt with it, or regift it as a **Perpetual Present** (which is always fun). You never know when you may run into someone who really would like it, so you might want to put it into your regift storage space for a while. Remember that somebody somewhere thought this was a good gift idea. And somebody actually bought it for *you*. (Or did they?) These gifts can be "interesting" and fun to regift with a sense of humor.

Best regifted to

- relatives,

- teachers,

- people you don't know very well, don't like very well, or will never see,

- anyone with a sense of humor.

Regifting Scenario

It looks like potpourri, smells like dirt, and comes in an odd-shaped ceramic thingy in "earth-tone hues to harmonize with any decor." Graciously regift it? Although it may be more fun to just give as is, try this instead. Write a "letter of tranquility" explaining that "having this curious piece of soothing artistry in your home can calm you on even your worst days if you close your eyes, inhale the earthy aroma of Mother Nature, and visualize yourself at one with the world." Add a "Sounds of Nature" CD or something similar. Peace.

#17 The Fab Find 🎁 🎁 🎁 🎁 🎁

Finding something rather cool, unique, and gift-worthy in the trash, on the ground, on the bus, etc., is always considered a good find. There is actually a lot of gracious regifting potential in these items, but it calls for an enormous amount of artistry and imagination. (Or you could just lie…)

As stated earlier with **BIBs**, you cannot actually regift something that you never received as a gift in the first place, but a **Fab Find** falls under the heading of Regift Exception #2. And as long as you are giving it to someone else under the pretense of it being something purchased by you exclusively for them, the regift is similarly categorized as a **Do-over**.

This is not a very common method of regifting, of course, but it can be one of the most fun, and it is actually one of my favorites. However, there are those few—and somewhat freaky!—family members and friends that are practically famous for searching for, and finding, funky and sometimes really funny stuff used only for regifting!

(Not to mention any names, but I do actually happen to be acquainted with a family like that, and I am really quite fond of them!)

Tips for Gracious Regifting
Once again, when attempting to regift any gift in this category, so much depends on what it is and who you will be regifting it to. This is another gift that goes great with a good story! You can, of course, personalize this **Fab**

Regift Exception #2

If an item made, found, or purchased was at some point previously used by, or intended for, yourself or anyone else, and you decide to give it as a gift to someone else, it is still regarded as a regift.

Find, embellish it a little, or repackage it up in a special way, any of which may seem less tacky and make you feel less guilty, if you actually do feel that way.

Best regifted to

- relatives,

- friends,

- co-workers,

- neighbors.

Regifting Scenario

While you are on your morning power walk, you spot a seems-to-be perfectly good, simple wooden desk chair by the road near someone's trash. Since you could use a desk chair, you go to get it. Upon closer inspection (you didn't have to be that close), you see that the seat is missing. It's a seemingly perfect seat-less chair. You, a Regifting Guru, know just what to do. You take the chair home, paint or stain it, and take some chicken wire and attach it to the "seat" of the chair so that it looks as if a bowl is sitting in it. Get some coconut moss (the thick, brown, furry stuff) and line the chicken-wire "bowl" with it. Fill it with potting soil, add some flowers or plants of your choice (regift the plant you got in the hospital?), and then you graciously regift this "blooming chair" to your new neighbor as a "Welcome!" gift for their porch, deck, or wherever.

Note: If you make perfectly clear that the gift you are graciously regifting *was actually found on the ground* (or wherever) and you make up a great story about why you felt compelled to give it to the recipient, and add in all the work you did to make it perfect for them, and they are *still thrilled* with their present, then you are truly a great Gracious Regifter!

#18 The Remarketer

Have you ever received a gift that is supposedly meant for a particular purpose, but you feel that the item has (regift) potential for other more suitable uses—but darn if they aren't any that *you* could use or need or would even want? The difference here from the **Alien** is that you actually know what this is.

Tips for Gracious Regifting

It takes very good sales skills and a good imagination to be able to pull off graciously regifting a useless item to the giftee by enthusiastically endorsing it as something he or she cannot possibly live without. Sometimes you may have to repackage a **Remarketer**, especially if the original package lists the actual (unusable) intended uses. Another way to graciously regift it would be to truly make it into something else entirely.

Best regifted to

- relatives,
- friends,

- co-workers,

- neighbors,

- anyone who will be convinced of its usefulness.

Regifting Scenario

Pour candle wax (just melt down a few of your old ones for a complete regift) into the lovely teapot you would never use (nor would anyone else) after placing a wick inside, and then graciously regift it as a unique candle for the kitchen. Plus, you get the bonus of the gift getter feeling all gooey because you took the time and trouble to make them a personal, one-of-a-kind gift! How cool is that?

#19 The TUI (pronounced "too ee")

At some point in life, everyone receives as a *gift* a **T**otally **U**seless **I**tem. Face it, there are some items you get from folks that are *so senseless* (to most of us, anyway, although somewhere someone must have thought it was a good idea!) that they are almost too pathetic to regift to anyone. At least, not to someone you know, like, and/or get paychecks from (relatives are excluded—in fact, most of these **TUIs** are given to us by our relatives!). Included in this category are some of those goodies and "gadgets" from catalogs that cater to the kind of people that truly think **TUIs** are totally cool and useful because, of course, they actually do like them and probably really use them! (Remember who these people are for gracious regifting to in the future...) These catalogs usually contain words like "unique," "unusual," and "hard-to-find, one-of-a-kind gifts" and contain "To Die For" items such as a "muscle man light switch," a two-toned fruit fondue set, a three-piece set of beehive mixing bowls, and a "swinging fairy" sculpture for your garden.

Additionally, in this category, you may want to consider joke or "gag gifts," especially those given on milestone birthdays, e.g., standard "Over The Hill" canes and "Old Fart" ball caps. The difference between these gifts and an **Alien** or the **Chronic Regift**, among others, is that you are likely to receive more than one **TUI** at a time, usually for the same occasion and likely from the same person or people. Sometimes they come in sets (the gifts, not the people). You could also regard these **TUIs** as Tacky, Useless & Inane; Totally & Unbelievably Inept; Tremendously Unusual & Indescribable; Too Unbelievably Idiotic...you get the picture!

These are usually the regiftables that are put into "Regift Starter Kits," taken to parties, or given when gifts get to be exchanged "anonymously." Or they get regifted as a joke or part of some other gift.

Tips for Gracious Regifting

There is really very little you can do to upgrade, alter, embellish, improve, or add to these gifts that would make them any more regiftable, unless you are *extremely* creative, have a terrific sense of humor, and the gift getter is worth the effort. You could incorporate the gift into another gift, or add some additional, similar **TUIs** as a type of a theme regift. You could also write a clever story, poem, letter; draw a picture, make papier-mâché people—add anything that explains(?) why you are giving (or regifting) this absurd gift or gifts. You could actually turn one or more **TUIs** into a witty gift for "the person who has everything" to make them realize that they really don't! Whether or not you choose to admit to graciously regifting is entirely up to you. It could be part of the fun, which is why **TUIs** can make terrific **Perpetual Presents**! However, some things are just better left unsaid (or perhaps simply kept for posterity!). On the other hand, if you keep the item long enough, maybe someday you might actually need it, or meet someone else who does!

> **Note:** If you can successfully graciously regift a **TUI**, wherein the gift getter is totally pleased and appreciative, you have achieved regifting grandeur! You should be so proud!

Best regifted to

- anyone you're brave enough—or skilled enough—to give it to,

- anyone who also has a sense of humor,

- a "Frequent Regifter" (seriously!),

- a relative,

- a neighbor you don't know…

Regifting Scenario

Create the perfect gift "For The Person Who Has Everything, But Apparently *Doesn't*" (or something like that). You can make it gender specific, if you have enough appropriate gifts, or generic. Use about four to twelve **TUIs**, or a significant number, like five for turning fifty. Using something besides a box or bag to put them in is good, like a laundry basket or other useful container. Write up a great story or poem for each item if you want, relating why you specifically "chose" the gifts for him or her, and/or their significance to the person or the occasion. You can label each one as well: "*Doesn't* have a Bushy Brows eyebrow trimmer"; "*Doesn't* have a bowling ball polishing cloth"; "*Doesn't* have static-free slippers," etc. This can be a good "group gift" for a milestone birthday or going-away party, retirement, etc. Fun stuff!

#20 Special Consideration Regifts (or SCRs)

So far, we have discussed in detail nineteen types of presents people are more prone to regift. There are still, however, a few types of gifts that may be gotten that are typically regarded as "not regiftable" from the get go. In most cases, the gift getter would just keep these types of gifts, but never actually use them. However, they can be and do sometimes get successfully regifted. These things, too, have their own little rules and some good suggestions for "How Not to Regift This," just in case the situation should otherwise warrant it. (Review Gracious Regifting Fundamental #2.) Depending on the circumstances and the quality of the gift to be regiven, any of these items could certainly qualify as "regiftable" under one of the other gracious regifting methods as well. Although many of these rules seem like "common sense," you might be surprised...So pay attention!

A. Gift Cards

On the rare occasion when you receive a gift card that you simply can not, will not, or would not want to use anywhere, you may decide to regift it (presumably to someone who will genuinely appreciate its product value). Note that we are referring to gift cards you have received as a gift, don't need or don't want, and are therefore graciously regifting them to someone else. A *new* gift card could also be purchased, and used, as an add-on to another gift you are regifting.

Tips for Gracious Regifting

A relatively recent option, the gift card regift must be handled very carefully. You can always add something to it, repackage it, or embellish it in creative ways, like wrapping it up with another gift (another regift?), or perhaps you could tuck it into a cute stuffed bear or a pocket on a wild-looking little T-shirt or some similar item. Make it fun!

There are also some things you should never do when regifting a gift card.

- Do not give a partially used gift card unless you change the amount that is written on the card, or recharge it. (It is a dead regift giveaway to receive a gift card worth $18.76.)

- Do not forge the actual amount of the card (like leaving the $20.00 written on the card when it is now only worth $18.76 and hope no one notices).

- Do not give a soon-to-expire gift card or forge the expiration date of the card (in the hope that they won't use it anyway).

- Do not give a gift card for something the recipient doesn't need or wouldn't/couldn't use, e.g., a twenty-five-dollar gift card to Wines R Us for an AA graduation gift (now you're a Regifting Goober *and* a jerk).

- Do not give a gift card or gift certificate for something that does not even exist within the city limits of the recipient.

- Do not give a gift card with a Christmas theme on it for a birthday in August, or one with a hologram of a baby for a wedding gift.

- Do not forget to cover up or somehow change the name and/or amount (if it is no longer correct) on the gift card. And don't *fail* in your attempt to try to cover up or cross out the original recipient and/or amount.

Best regifted to
- generally anyone, especially anyone you know who is fond of the specific card merchant.

Regifting Scenario
If you are regifting a gift card from a local coffee shop, put it in a coffee or travel mug (one of your regiftables?). A gift card from a women's clothing store could be graciously regifted tucked inside of a fashion doll outfit.

B. Food Items

Boxes of candy, cans of cookies, bottles of wine and other spirits, as well as gourmet specialty items also make great items to regift. "Food towers" fall into this category as well. Ordinarily you get these specialty shop and food catalog items from well-meaning friends, relatives, and business associates. Baskets of fruit, tins of truffles, strange kinds of crackers, sausage logs, petit fours, lots of meat rolls, and tubs or tubes of funky-flavored cheeses and spreads—they all make great "hostess gifts" to graciously regift when you are invited to a party! And if they come with neat boxes or other unusual but definitely reusable containers, you can save those and reuse them for repackaging other gifts. If food items are part of a set, e.g., an electric bun warmer filled with biscuit mixes, then you may already have a **2fer** or a **Partial Gift** regift ready to go!

In addition, what about those food items, sets, and mixes you receive due to hosting and/or attending those popular parties that feature and promote "fine foods" that come in resealable boxes and bags? (Some items even include handy kitchen gadgets that you will never need, and they can also be graciously regifted.) Even if you have probably bought some of these products simply to satisfy your obligation to attend, at least you can graciously regift them to someone else. (Just make sure the person that you regift to was not also at the party.)

And don't forget those plates, trays, and jars of holiday treats and baked goods from your neighbors. Just turn right around and take them to another party—as long as it is not in your same neighborhood. (Really, it's not such a bad thing, especially if they are still warm!)

Tips for Gracious Regifting

Before regifting food items, make sure you always check for expiration dates on the items. You don't want to make people ill with your well-intended regifts. It is also possible that the person who brought it to you regifted it themselves! After that, try the following to add a more personal touch to your regifted "homemade" food item:

- Prepare the item (as directed) before you leave and present it as "homemade" (you don't think people do this already?). Don't forget to put your name somewhere on the dish you bring it in to add to its authenticity, or bring it in something that you don't need returned. (Another regift?)

- Re-garnish and regift the homemade cheese log that Aunt Mary gave to you at Christmas by removing the little mistletoe decoration and sticking a mini football on it instead. You can feel perfectly okay with bringing it to that Super Bowl party, and you could even buy a box of crackers to add to the regift (or just use some from your pantry).

- Remove the "Made Especially for You by …" or "From the Kitchen of …" stickers on the item, or just replace them with your own! You may want to have a supply of personalized stickers just for these occasions. On the other hand, you could leave the original stickers on and just graciously regift it as if it really *was* made especially for them. So what if they don't know who Aunt Betty is.

- Repackage the item in a unique bag, or box, and decorate or embellish it (such as plopping a fresh pile of whipped topping on the Jell-O salad leftover from your church potluck). Or make up a great story as to the significance of the item to the occasion. ("I noticed you eating several pieces of key lime pie at my last party, so I made one for you!" Be sure to remove it from the box before you thaw it out.)

- Rewrap homemade breads, muffins, brownies, fudge, and candy previously brought to you and tie it up with a pretty ribbon or bow, adding a new tag. One year I received four different kinds of pound cakes, and so with a little ingenuity, and some holiday plastic wrap, I had four perfectly good gifts to give to guests at my holiday dinner. I also recommend sharing your baked good gifts by splitting them up between you and the giftee. You keep a fair amount of the food, and you divvy the rest up for regifting. Presenting it on a pretty plate or a decorative storage tub (that was also a gift) that can be kept by the giftee allows you to enjoy some stuff for yourself and still graciously regift without anyone being the wiser. (Plus, it's one less regiftable item you have to hang on to.) This is especially helpful if you do not bake and you receive an abundant amount of holiday cookies arranged tastefully (no pun here) on a pretty plate from your neighbors or co-workers. Just keep the snickerdoodles and regift the rest.

Best regifted to

- hosts/hostesses of dinners or parties you are invited to,

- teachers (but stick to non-perishables),

- neighbors (especially at holiday times),

- your boss and co-workers,

- friends (under certain circumstances, e.g., they really like what you don't or they are sick and it will be healing...)

Regifting Scenario

Your neighbor brings over a dozen donuts in the morning, just because, and you take them into the teacher's lounge at your son's school later that morning "from you" (after nuking them for a few moments to warm and freshen them up). And the jelly-of-the-month membership that you got from your boss has been a godsend to graciously regift to the current Bunko hostess each month (wrapped in a colorful tea towel).

C. Seasonal Stuff

At holiday times, especially around Christmas, Easter, and whatever other religious, cultural, or ethnic holidays you celebrate, it seems as though some people feel obligated to give you gifts that you can only use during the particular season in which they were given. Eventually, you can build up quite the collection of seasonal stuff. Now if you actually use these items, e.g., for decorating, adorning your own home or office, and for holiday entertaining, then you are probably much more appreciative of them. There really are those who willingly collect seasonal items, are actually giddy to get them, anxious to use them, and are always on the lookout for more.

But perhaps you are not one of them. Do you find yourself on the receiving end of various festive serving platters, candles, bathroom commode sets, appliance covers, and dishtowels depicting specific holidays and/or characters associated with such? And what about all of the other adorable decorative items you repeatedly receive *that you will never use*? Why do

Regifting Revival!
Jodi Newbern

you keep hauling them out of the attic every year, only to add more unused and unwanted items to the already overstuffed boxes of baubles and hoist them back up to the attic again till next year? Well, now you know that you can graciously regift them!

Tips for Gracious Regifting

It is perfectly acceptable and common to graciously regift seasonable items when they are currently "in season." If you wait until later in the season to regift, you will probably have more inventory from which to choose. It's usually good to "group up" several of these items together and graciously regift them, which has the added benefit of keeping your regiftable supply low. Unless the seasonal item you are regifting is something that the giftee specifically wanted, e.g., an addition to a set they already have or a collectible, it is difficult and not very popular to regift seasonable items during "off season." (However, it is a great time to stock up on them to regift later, especially if you enjoy graciously regifting **BIBs**.)

Best regifted to

- relatives (unless they gave it to you),

- teachers,

- your boss,

- co-workers,

- neighbors,

- friends.

Regifting Scenario

Purchase a lot of Christmas ornaments at 50 percent off to give to everyone next year as your "signature gift." (If you are really "gracious," embellish them a little or write names on them.) Taking the Santa spoons you got from your chiropractor December 10 and graciously regifting them to your podiatrist December 15 is ideal (unless they are in the same practice). Easter baskets can be regifted with other items throughout the year as add-ons, enhancements, or repackaging—but be sure to remove the grass first (and stray jellybeans), and be conscious of the basket color.

D. Clothing and Shoes

One would consider the regifting of any wearable item questionable and best left as donations to thrift shops or other charities if they are not returnable. But as with most everything else, there are a few notable exceptions. Sometimes there is no accounting for taste, and often that is the case when receiving clothing or shoes as a gift. And in this case, refer also to Regift Exception #2. Additionally, major weight changes, incorrect sizing, the season, and tastes that may radically differ from the gift giver can account for clothing items being considered regiftable.

Tips for Gracious Regifting

As with jewelry, it is better if the item has never been worn (except possibly when briefly wearing it for the thank-you photo, which you will learn about later). Even better if it still has the original tags. However, if it has been "gently worn"—at least long enough to realize you don't want it for whatever reason—and it's still in "near enough to perfect" condition, it is acceptable to graciously regift. (A handmade item may fall under the list of Regifting Faux Pas, so proceed with caution.) Make sure that you thoroughly check the item for any flaws, especially if it may have been purchased at a discount due to its "slightly irregular" status. In the case where the item may have been briefly worn (especially if you have been seen wearing it), remove any pet hairs, offensive odors, or "suspicious stains" unless it may have some significant or even historic value, such as a blue dress worn to visit the President. It might be considered an heirloom, or sometimes the item may have been intended to be humorous or given purposely as a joke. In that case, you could also graciously regift it as a **Do-Over**, a **Remarketer**, or a **Perpetual Present**.

Best regifted to

- very close friends and relatives who have different tastes but would truly appreciate the item,

- friends and relatives who are not that close, and you don't really know if they would appreciate it or not, nor do you really care,

- friends and relatives who would appreciate the humor (if intended as such).

Regifting Scenario

The "Box of Chocolates a Day" diet didn't work out too well for you, so you no longer have need for your brand-new, pre-diet size ten "Weekend Wardrobe" purchased just for your planned vacation. Now that you are a svelte size sixteen, it is no longer likely that you could actually "Wear It Fifty Ways!" so why not graciously regift it to your friend (who chose a different weight-loss regime that actually worked) who is vacationing with you? A "congratulatory" gift or a "bon voyage" present would be so thoughtful. Include a really large box of chocolates for a sweet touch.

E. Jewelry

Jewelry is tough to give as a gift anyway, unless you are very close to the recipient, because it can have an intimate connotation to some. So if you decide to regift it, make sure you are graciously regifting it to someone who would really appreciate it and would really want to wear it. Of course, the (perceived) value of the jewelry will also have an impact on its regiftability, but since it is doubtful that anyone would actually attempt to regift genuinely valuable baubles—unless you reside in Beverly Hills—for the sake of argument, we will presume costume jewelry.

Tips for Gracious Regifting

- It's better if it has not been worn; however, if it has only been "gently used" and still looks shiny and new, it could probably pass. Also, make sure it is actually what you say it is. (If you say it is 14-carat gold, it had really better be!)

- You might want to keep a couple of those little boxes jewelry comes in on hand, along with the cotton strips or the fasteners that keep them in the boxes. If it actually is brand-new, of course, you can use the original packaging, or you may want to be creative and clever and put the jewelry in, on, or around something instead of a box (unless you are using a Tiffany's box for a non-Tiffany piece). Using a baby doll that is sporting some sterling silver chains around its neck, for example, will definitely get you the "wow factor" for your regift.

- Do not try to pass off old rings and earrings as heirlooms, or any jewelry given to you by young children or your spouse (unless they are no longer such). Trust us on this one.

Best regifted to

- relatives,

- close friends,

- close co-workers.

Regifting Scenario

If regifting a pair of (fake) diamond stud earrings, stick them into the ears of a stuffed animal—which, by the way, works well for regifting other types of jewelry as well. Other unique packaging could find jewelry graciously regifted inside coffee cans, ornaments, mini-stockings, and plastic eggs.

F. Books

It is not as odd as you might think. The only tricky part about graciously regifting books is deciding on whether or not your giftee would even like or appreciate it. Adults will want books they have not yet read, but want to. Collector's books, comic books, first editions, "family" books, cartoon books, cookbooks, coffee table books, and gift books (this book...) also make good regifts. Children's books are much easier to regift, as long as no pages have been ripped out, chewed, or scribbled on.

Tips for Gracious Regifting

- If the book is brand-new, meaning you have not already read that particular copy, then there is no problem regifting it if you just are not interested in it. However, make sure that it is not personally inscribed to you (or anyone else!).

- If you have read that particular copy, or suspect that someone else already has—and you still want to regift it—make sure the spine is not wrinkled or worn, and all bookmarks, paper clips, and photos of your kids are removed.

- Check for spots, stains, or water-warped pages or covers. And crumbs (some people eat while they read).

- Make sure there are no torn, bent, highlighted, underlined, or missing pages.

- For heaven's sake, make sure it's a title that is from this decade, or is considered a classic, and is one that your giftee might actually want to read. A good-as-new copy of *Valley Of The Baby Dolls* probably won't be well received.

- You might consider including a personalized bookmark, bookplate, and/or an inscription on the inside cover. (Of course, that would keep your giftee from regifting it again.) If there is already an inscription, please do not try to write over it, cover it up, or change the name or the date. (That actually would be tacky.)

- Add-ons like bookmarks, book lights, bookends, bookstands, bookcases, etc., are always good. For "theme" books, adding to them with like items, e.g., a singing fish with a copy of *The Family Fishing Guide* definitely makes it a gracious regift. (See Regift Exception #3.)

Best regifted to
- anyone who likes books!

Regifting Scenario

Graciously regift *Tommy the Tank—The Complete Set* (that your kids never missed) with a toy tank, a "TTT" official sticker book, or a pair of "Tommy" no-skid slipper socks.

G. Perfume, Cologne, Body sprays, etc. 🎁 🎁 🎁

I would not regift these to just anyone unless you don't care. Like jewelry, you should make sure it would be appreciated, as it is also a tough regift unless you really know what your giftee likes (perfumes and colognes are a very personal choice).

Tips for Gracious Regifting

Unlike jewelry, perfumes cannot be "gently used." If you have used it, you can keep it. But they are okay if they have never been used or are in a set, and especially if they come with some free soap or lotion (but then that could be a **2fer**, a **Partial Gift**, or a **Freebie**). This is the same for body sprays. They are better as add-ons with other regifts; to graciously regift them alone you'll want to repackage them. Unless it comes in its own little gift box, you can repackage it in just about anything, as long as it has never been opened. Sometimes, when these items come in "gift sets" with other items, you can graciously regift them like a **2fer** or a **Freebie**.

Best regifted to
- relatives,
- friends,

- teachers (sorry, Teach!),

- co-workers.

Regifting Scenario

If you received a bottle of perfume or cologne you don't want, you are sure that your giftee likes the particular scent, and you do not want to add in or add on, then you'll just have to find a classy way to graciously regift it other than simply wrapping it up or stuffing it into a gift bag. If you have a cardboard poster tube, stuff one end with tissue paper, drop in the bottle (you may want to wrap it in paper or tissue first), toss in some wrapped chocolates if you have some, stuff the rest with tissue paper, and wrap or decorate the tube. You could personalize it if you are so inclined. Make your gift getter guess what is in the tube. (They probably won't, but at least you'll find out what poster they really wanted and thought that they were getting.)

Regift Exception #3

If a newly purchased item is given as part of a gift along with a regiftable item, or a regiftable item is part of a gift that also includes a newly purchased item, whether simply for add-on or enhancement purposes, the entire gift is still considered a regift.

H. Toys

There is really no way to graciously regift a board game, or any game, actually, unless you have never played it and all of the pieces are still wrapped in plastic. Otherwise, you will probably have to admit regift on this one. It will likely be obvious, and I don't think you could talk your way around it, unless the giftee wouldn't care, or if you tell them how difficult it was to get, how long it took you to find it, and how all of the "trouble was worth it" because you knew they really wanted it...if indeed they actually did.

Tips for Gracious Regifting

Assuming a board game was only played once and no one liked it, the only way to graciously regift it is to give it to someone you played it with who actually thought it was a blast—regift it quick before they buy their own. Regifting a brand-new grown-up toy is pretty much like giving a new gift. However, good luck trying to regift a brand-new kids' toy unless your kid doesn't want it, or does not remember that he got it. (A great tactic to use when you have a birthday party with twenty-five kids—and twenty-five more gifts that your child does not need—is to quickly stash all of the stuff you don't want, or don't want your kid to have, like the toy F-18 Super Hornet "With Real Jet Sound!") As long as the child getting the regift doesn't know any different, you'll be fine. However, be aware that kids are much more likely to spot a regift than adults are. And there is nothing more embarrassing than being called out by a kid. (For instance, after your kid's party you quickly put away half of his gifts, and then later you slyly rewrap one for him to take to another kid's party, but when the other kid opens the present, *your* kid cries, "Hey! That's mine—I got that!" The only thing that would actually be more embarrassing is if the kid that got the regift was the same kid who gave it to your kid in the first place!)

You can also regift toys like a **BIB**, except now the **BIB** is an excess of kid's books, toys, games, dolls, cars, or coloring stuff you bought on sale that you keep hidden away for the weekly birthday parties your little darlings will be invited to attend beginning at age one, or whenever they go to school (whichever comes first).

Best regifted to

- adults,

- children,

- anyone who likes games and toys.

Regifting Scenario

You and some friends played "Basements and Attics" all night long—only because your friends thought it was great. You didn't, so guess what they are going to get? Carefully put all the pieces back in the game, use snack baggies if you already threw out the original plastic. Since they already know it's a regift, and assuming they don't care, you should still think of an inventive way to graciously regift it to them. If you have a warehouse store in your vicinity, see if you can find the largest snack canister—or any large reusable container that the game box will fit into (even a dog food or kitty litter canister). The idea is to place the game at the bottom and fill it up with snacks—wrapped ones, hopefully, so you don't get ick all over the game (great if you found one already full of snacks; otherwise, dump out and clean out thoroughly the dog food, kitty litter, or detergent bucket).

Wrap or decorate the container or not—if you can make up a creative use for the plastic "bucket" later, even better.

I. Video Games, CDs, and DVDs

Similarly, as in the regifting of books, video games, CDs, and DVDs should also be in new or near-perfect condition, preferably not pre-played, and still in original shrink-wrap and/or packaging. However, with the popularity of purchasing "previously used" games, videos, and audios, if you are positive that it's something the gift getter would really appreciate getting, then go ahead and graciously regift it to them.

Tips for Gracious Regifting

You could insert a (re)gift card from an appropriate store into the "previously used" case or give a toy musical instrument with the CD or a movie-theme-related item with the DVD, etc. It's your call whether or not you confess to its secondhand status, but if the label on the disc says "Property of Broadway Babes Video Club," you probably don't want to keep it a secret.

Best regifted to

- anyone who plays video games, watches movies, or listens to music.

Regifting Scenario

If you are clever enough to actually graciously regift a previously used/owned game/DVD/CD, knowing that your giftee will not care, you could always replace the original box with another box, preferably with the cover or title of something that is totally the opposite of what is really inside, or that your giftee would appreciate. This is funny when you put an action-packed "bombs, blood, and broads" movie in a sappy "chick flick" box, or an Englebert Humperdinck case with a "Rhinestones & Road Kill" CD inside. They won't even think about the fact that it's a regift.

J. Power Tools, Electronics, and Small Appliances 🎁 🎁 🎁 🎁

You probably assumed that these items were off limits as far as regifting goes, didn't you? (Remember what happens when one assumes…) But the truth is, now that housewarming and retirement parties, along with wedding showers (for the couple, and also more recently for the groom), are becoming acceptable, as well as the more traditional showers for babies and brides-to-be, the possibility of getting a number of duplicate and/or unnecessary gifts is highly likely. Not usually chainsaws, plasma TVs, or dorm refrigerators, but potential regiftables like cordless drills, handheld Sudoku games, and onion blossom makers. Sometimes the items are just slightly out of date, so it is rather obvious it's a regift, e.g., SaladShooters, Hot Doggers, and personal cassette players. (If you have never heard of these items, then you get the point.) They are most likely gifts that you could have returned—but didn't. Nevertheless, they, too, can be graciously regifted in the right situation. Actually, most people don't mind getting these types of gifts, even if they suspect they are regifts. At least they are generally useful.

Tips for Gracious Regifting

As with most other gifts that you want to graciously regift, you must make sure that they are in great condition. Using the regifting ideas from the **IDer**, the **Fab Find**, and the **Remarketer** (or any of them that may apply), be sure to be clear with your giftee of your reasons for regifting, unless you want your regift to be considered "new," as most actually are.

When regifting a "gently used" camera or personal CD player, for example (just because you got a better camera and an iPod), make sure that any film, photos, or music is removed before repackaging. It is also best to take out the batteries and give a pack of *new* batteries with the regift. If you are really a Gracious Regifter, whether the item is new or not so new, including new batteries, film, or a CD with it is always a good idea.

Best regifted to
- friends,
- relatives,
- neighbors,
- someone getting married, moving, or furnishing a vacation home,
- anyone with ample storage space.

Regifting Scenario
You have one too many slow cookers (how many does the average citizen need, anyway?), so you'll need to graciously regift at least one of them.

It's best to make sure your giftee doesn't already have one, to increase their appreciation of the gift. To graciously regift it, add a cookbook, or the potholders/dishtowel set with the apples that you got from a long-ago neighbor. It will make a great wedding gift.

K. Plants and Flowers

Regifting flowers is best done with those contained in pots or planters. You really cannot regift cut or fresh flowers unless you regift them on the very same day—possibly the next day—that you got them, unless it's really the container or vase that is the regift. Make sure you remove or exchange the card. Also, make sure the giftee even likes plants (some people don't possess any for a reason—like having black thumbs, or deadly allergies). If the flowers or plants are from a funeral home or hospital room, the gift getter *must* be told, especially if they aren't (if you will excuse the pun) as fresh as daisies. Do not attempt to regift flowers or plants that are wilted, dying, dead, or ugly. (This goes without saying, but you never know…)

Tips for Gracious Regifting

Plants are graciously regifted by adding something to them or sticking some type of decoration in the planter. Assuming you're regifting on the same day, flowers are graciously regiftable when you wrap them up as a bouquet, place them in a different vase, add something to them, or re-arrange them. If possible, just keep the flowers or plants that you get, but then use the vase or container for regifting something else later. It will be much safer. Here are a few tips on who not to regift to:

- Do not attempt to regift flowers or plants *to* your wife that were from your neighbor, mistress, secretary, or girlfriend (even if they are one and the same).

- Do not attempt to regift flowers or plants that were *from* your husband or children to your pool boy, neighbor, or boyfriend (even if they are one and the same).

- Do not attempt to regift flowers to your girlfriend/boyfriend, husband, or wife from *anyone* for any reason. Period. (Plants could probably pass, but most likely you will be grilled about "where did this come from?")

Best regifted to (be mindful of the rules...)
- relatives,

- teachers,

- neighbors,

- sick friends,

- not your boss.

Regifting Scenario

If you have a regiftable glass bowl, you can fill it with colored marbles, add water to it, cut the stems of the prettiest flowers down to about six inches or so, depending on the depth of your bowl, and stick the flowers into the marbles any way you want. You can also snip the stems off completely and "float" the flower tops in the bowl. If you add lemon-lime soda to the water, it will help them to keep longer. This could be graciously regifted as a birthday gift or taken to a dinner at a friend's house.

"All's fair in love and regifting."

~regifting proverb

4 GUARANTEEING A GREAT REGIFT

As you know, there will always be those few lousy, renegade regifters who will continue to be portrayed as "People With Poor Taste," only being invited to lame birthday parties held in damp basements and bowling alleys. They are perfectly okay being referred to as tawdry gift givers, capable only of regifting their cheesy, stupid, peculiar, lame, unwanted, unneeded, tacky, and useless gifts to the most innocent and unsuspecting people on the planet. They really want us true Gracious Regifters to be kept out of the limelight, instead of getting much-deserved kudos for our significant contributions to ecology.

> **Regifting is the #1 way to recycle unwanted gift waste!**

It is vital to our economy, our country, and our credit cards that all of the unwanted stuff that we have accumulated in our closets can finally be graciously regifted to almost anyone without feeling any more guilt!

Gracious Regifting Fundamental #3

It really can be better to give than to receive. (Just as long as you don't try to deceive.) It is even better to regift—graciously, of course!

To that end, this chapter is dedicated to the steps necessary to ensure the complete gracious regifting experience. If it is true that people hate what they fear, and fear what they do not understand, then we have to teach these clever and tasteful regifting tricks to all gift givers and gift getters everywhere! We will continue to train those who are willing to become Gracious Regifters, no matter what kinds of gifts they are giving, what kinds of gifts that they got, no matter from whom or where they got them from, or to whom they will be giving them again. Absolute education and outstanding communication are what we need.

Always Say "Thank You" (Even if You Intend to Regift It)

"Graciously regift unto others as you would have others graciously regift unto you."

~the "golden regift rule"

While knowing how to graciously regift an unwanted gift you have received is the core element to our Regifting Revival mission, it is equally important to know how to graciously *receive* a regift. Especially since giving—and getting—regifts will soon become commonplace in our communities, we need to become just as comfortable with receiving gifts being regifted to us. Setting the example of total acceptance toward gracious regifting as it pertains to gift getting, as well as to gift giving, is truly "putting our regift where our mouth is." The more comfortable and competent we get in our gracious regifting, and the more we spread the word, then ultimately receiving regifts should be just as satisfactory as receiving any types of gifts. Many people, after expressing their unwavering support for gracious regifting in general, tend to have a slightly different opinion when they are on the receiving end of the regift exchange. It will take time to rid ourselves of our prejudices, but in the meantime, the more regifts you graciously give, the more you should theoretically get back. Isn't that what our "regifting revival" is all about, anyway? Any and all

I

Really

Enjoy

Getting regifts

It's

Fun,

Too!

gifts should be appreciated, no matter if it's a regift or not, and no matter how "regiftable" it is.

Now, when you do receive a gift that is, indeed, somewhat odd, "unique," or unusual (or absolutely unusable) that you probably will want to give to someone else at some other time, there is something important that you might want to do before you stow it away, or ready it for regifting.

Have a picture or two taken of yourself with the gift: holding it, hugging it, using it, displaying it, or wearing whatever it was that you got. (A short video is effective, too.) Send the photo(s) to the gift giver, along with your thoughtful thank-you note. (Yes, even regiftable gifts certainly deserve this nicety, especially if you are a genuine Gracious Regifter.) That way, the gift giver will always think that you really were truly enamored with their clever contribution to your regiftable bounty. This idea can be especially impactful if you live far away from the friend (or relative) who was so sincere in their gift selection. (Or when you find yourself stuck with an **Alien**, **ASOTI**, **Perpetual Present**, **Chronic Regift**, or **TUI**...)

Additionally, a sincere Gracious Regifter will make an effort to have a local gift giver see you using, wearing, and/or displaying their gift to you (at least once) before you regift it. Even if it means inviting them to your house just to see how the lovely candle set enclosed in the gilded birdcage hanging in your foyer enhances your home's ambiance, just as they said it would. (The next time they visit, it's in the guest room if they ask…but you might want to have a photo ready.)

Regifting Faux Pas and Other Ways to Ruin (or Remake) Your Regifter Reputation

Any self-respecting Gracious Regifter knows that, although there may be a tendency to consider all gifts gotten as potential regifts, the fact is, *there are some gifts that simply will not be regifted.* (Remember the most pertinent rule in regifting: *"Almost any gift can be regifted…"*?)

But, as in all noble endeavors, especially for those who are still not quite used to this unique enterprise, there is a window of tolerance. In the beginning, when you are a novice regifter, you may make a few mistakes. That's okay as long as you learn from them. In order for you to maintain a favorable regifting grade amongst your family and friends, there are a few serious slips that you will want to avoid. It may be in your favor to refer to this list often so as not to err unnecessarily in your early attempts to become a Gracious Regifter. Nothing worthwhile is ever easy, and learning to become a Gracious Regifter is no exception.

Before you set a gift aside to be regifted, it is always a good idea to stick a note with the date and name of the giver on the gift somewhere, or to keep some sort of a log. In part 5 we have included a Regift Inventory Log Template just for that purpose; using it is strongly encouraged!

⊘ *NEVER regift a gift back to the original gift giver (unless doing so for devious reasons, or for fun, as with a **Perpetual Present**). If you are not sure whom it came from, regift it only to someone that you barely know or rarely see (or really don't like very much).*

⊘ *NEVER regift a gift in a situation where the original gift giver may be present, or may learn of the regifting, unless you are prepared to concoct a thoroughly convincing story about "duplicates," or "I loved mine so much I thought you would want one, too…" You should practice saying these statements until they sound natural, or you actually believe them. Sometimes this happens accidentally, but it may still have adverse effects…*

⊘ *NEVER forget to check the item thoroughly to make sure all cards, tags, or signs of previous ownership are removed, and/ or properly concealed (See the **IDer**). If you are regifting in the original packaging, i.e., gift-wrap or bag, be sure that it is relevant to the gift-giving occasion. (For example, if you are* *regifting a gift from a baby shower to someone getting married, definitely swap out the "It's A Boy!" gift-wrap for one that is more appropriate.)*

⊘ *NEVER regift anything given to you by your children, unless they are old enough to regift something from you. Remember that turnabout is fair play, and all is fair in love and regifting! This includes all artwork, clay dishware, popsicle stick pencil holders, anything imprinted with "I Love You," and "real" jewelry from their elementary school store.*

⊘ *NEVER regift a handcrafted afghan, sweater, housecoat, etc., made for you by a superannuated relative, neighbor, or friend while they are still among us. (Any time after their time, openly regifting it as an heirloom is acceptable.)*

⊘ *NEVER regift an item that is exclusively individualized, or is part of a "secret" or "inside joke," or perhaps is actually an authentic family heirloom (unless you are only "passing it on" to another family member).*

⊘ *NEVER regift an item given to you accompanied by a great story or anecdote, especially if it has personal meaning.*

⊘ *NEVER regift an item that is given in the spirit of sentimentality, especially if it is something truly intimate (This does not apply if the gift giver is no longer considered "intimate").*

○ *NEVER brag about your regifting skills or discuss the regifting opportunities to the giver of a gift you just received, or comment about the gifts' regifting potential in front of a person to whom you may possibly regift it to, unless they, too, are an experienced and Gracious Regifter. At least not until nearly everyone approves of this practice, or no one else is around.*

○ *NEVER forget to be mindful of the (ignorant) people who will never be comfortable with the concept of regifting, no matter how graciously done, and that they must be regifted to with caution. Perhaps they always really do want to keep whatever gifts come their way, and truly are appreciative of them all. However, more likely, the reason is based on their fear of being "found out," and the ensuing humiliation and ridicule they assume they will receive for their attempt at graciously regifting...*

Think Outside the (Regift) Box: Adding to, Enhancing, Embellishing, and Repackaging Regifts

If you are not yet completely comfortable with the idea of gracious regifting, don't worry. All it takes is a little practice. At first, you may want to only try regifting to your family and fake friends until you "get the hang of it."

You will probably feel a little funny about regifting most gifts exactly the way in which you received them. In most cases, when you are planning to regift, you will want to add a little something to the regift to make it truly an "original." For most regiftables, in order to make them as acceptable and as appropriate as possible for the person receiving the gift, the only option for successful gracious regifting it is to add to it, enhance it, embellish it, or repackage the gift. You cannot be too creative!

It is universally understood (or it soon will be), that as a Gracious Regifter, it is good practice to always give a regift better than how you received it.

Adding to a regift just means that you can put in some additional items (related or not, regiftable or not) to make it a more "complete" regift before you wrap it or stick it into a gift bag. (Remember Regift Exception #3.) Putting together a couple of candles, some massage oil (unopened, of course), and a romantic CD

Gracious Regifting Fundamental #4

As a Gracious Regifter, it is good practice to always give a regift better than how you received it.

could make a nice "couple's gift." Sometimes combining several gifts together in some sort of theme can work wonderfully as a gracious regift and could become a classic (or else continue into regift infinity, as with a **Chronic Regift**, or regifted again just for fun, as with a **Perpetual Present**!)

Combine one gift with another similar gift for a regift set. They don't have to know. If you ever receive a "Harvest Swag" (like

I have), you could pair it with the "Fall Foliage" fake flower arrangement (that I also received another time), and perhaps also throw in your never-used set of Pilgrim salt and pepper shakers for a wonderful way to help someone celebrate the first feast.

Using your assortment of seasonal items can be a plus for holiday gift giving, or for those folks lucky enough to celebrate pre-holiday birthdays. It's easy to put together a regift "snowman set" with several items from your stash.

Keep a supply of the "little" items you got from other gifts that would be too tacky to regift by themselves, e.g., the bottle stopper you got with a wine opener, and the wine glass markers that came with a bottle of vino you received. Those items could be put together and graciously regifted with a set of wine glasses (that you probably have several of).

When you **enhance a regift**, not only are you helping to "increase its worth" as a regift, but sometimes the item alone is better off, no matter who you regift it to. You don't necessarily need to be all that creative or inventive to enhance a gift. Nor do you need to enhance the regift with a lot of superfluous froufrou to make it acceptable. An enhancement is just a few little details that help personalize your regift and make it a little more special for the gift getter.

- Fix it up a little. Even just adding an engraved name or monogram can make a difference.

- Once again, composing a poem, a story, or a song about the regift can be effective. You do not have to overdo it, and it does not always have to be Nobel Prize worthy because of its ingenuity.

- Instead of simply regifting some of the picture frames you have received, graciously regift them with a meaningful photo. Even an unusual greeting card or postcard can be framed for a unique gift.

- Take a pair of those wine glasses from your regiftables, and graciously regift them with the tabletop wine rack, or wooden wine basket you had previously received. Add a bottle of "Cheap Red Wine" and "Cheap White Wine" and you have a terrific wedding or Anniversary gift.

Embellishing a regift is more detailed and "artistic" than simply enhancing your regift. And, it's great because you can actually make yourself (and others) believe that you are really giving a "virgin gift" and that you took the time and trouble to put it together and personalize it for the lucky regiftee. Decorating a plain glass bowl you got a while back could still be a lot better than buying a new one. Often, if you decide to acknowledge your regift as such, your gift getter will be so awed by your originality that it won't even matter.

Fix it up—a lot. Some stuff like garden gnomes, wind chimes, and heavy doorstops shaped like boots can actually become heirloom items if they are properly graciously regifted. Find and clean off the other cast iron "boot" you are using to weigh down the towering stack of newspapers in your garage (another recycling project you're working on), decorate them with acrylic paints—maybe a "his and hers" theme—and graciously regift an artsy-fartsy matched set of hand-painted bookends.

Sometimes you can take a really cheap or "unusual" item you have received, as with a **Do-over**, or purchased "previously owned" as with a **Fab Find**, and create a customized gift that could actually become a must-have item for all that see it! I once found a brand-new-looking Elvis change purse in a parking lot. Of course, I picked it up, and later found out a friend of mine who was having a birthday soon, was a true Elvis fan. I cleaned it up, attached it to a little blue suede shoe found in a thrift shop, and regifted it (see Regift Exception #2) to my friend, who was thrilled.

Just use your imagination. Even if all of your "artistic talent" is comparable to that of a three-year-old, just go with it. Maybe your work will look so incredibly juvenile that your gift getter will think it is deliberate or some kind of modern art piece. (Those boot bookends sure looked like a "real child" had painted them, and they were a hit.)

Do not underestimate the influence that **new (and improved) packaging** can do for a regift. Sometimes that can be more impressive than the regift itself! Great gift bags, gift boxes, shoes, and other accessories, old or new, can increase the viability of the gracious regift. Your creativity and inventiveness definitely count here, especially if this is the only "improvement" you are making to your regift!

- Make sure you have an ample supply of good tools and accessories for repackaging. Stock up on wrapping paper, tissue paper, ribbons, bows, stickers, cellophane wrapping, and shrink-wrap.

Note: If you recycle packaging items from other gifts you have received, e.g., wrapping and tissue paper, gift bags, etc., then you will not necessarily want to use them again for regifts. However, using recycled paper, bags, boxes, and bows on *virgin* gifts is acceptable and still "green" of you. While it does not mean that your new gift is a regift, using previously used packaging stuff still qualifies you as a regifter, no matter what anyone else says. And you know you've done it. So there!

- Just for fun, you can use various used and/or unusual boxes and bags for your gifts, like stuffing a silk scarf into a cereal box, or using empty CD/DVD/game cases to hold a (re)gift card from the related retail store. Anything can become a "container" for a regift. It is really all about being resourceful, and so you'll want to use, or recycle, whatever you have, right?

Take advantage of various items you might have gotten with gifts that you have previously received to use for regift repackaging, e.g., decorative tins (that often come with food items), vases and pots from flowers and plants, little boxes that jewelry came in, and even baskets and bowls from other gifts may be reused for regifting. You may also want to keep on hand some dollar store or other inexpensive items for creatively repackaging your regift and making it uniquely from you, such as little ceramic boxes, pretty vases, and picture frames. You want the giftee to be impressed, right?

What to Do with Your Gold Mine of Regiftables: Creating a Custom Regift Closet

Well, by now you have probably realized that you already do have, or soon really could have, enough stuff to start your own "Regift Closet"—or chest or cabinet or shelf or drawer or bag or box or bin. Use whatever you have the space for, wherever you have the space for it, to store whatever stuff you have. It is okay to start small since, if you are serious about setting up a separate section just for storing your regiftables, you will just keep adding on as needed. If you are "lucky" enough to receive a great amount

of regiftable gifts, and you are open to the gracious regifting practices we now have made you aware of, you will be upgrading your "gold mine of regiftables" in no time!

As you have learned, one of the reasons to regift something you have been given is not always because the gift is something that you would never consider keeping. Many times, especially among friends—and yes, even from some relatives (surprise!)—you will receive a gift that you actually do like and really would use sometime. Maybe it is something you *might even one day* need. However, you just do not need it *now*. On the other hand, it could be the gift was given to you because *someone else* was convinced you needed it—even if you did not know that you did.

This actually does happen a lot with friends and family—they love to give you things *they* think you need and want...even when you tell them otherwise. Families are especially fond of this kind of passive-aggressive gift giving. Example: (your mother) "It looks like you could really use a set of casserole covers." (You) "Actually, no, Mom, I don't ever make casseroles." And when the next gift-giving holiday comes along, guess what is wrapped up for you? Yep, a beautiful set of casserole covers! (Hopefully they are not monogrammed—and you know that she quite possibly scoured scores of yard sales before she found the perfect set...)

It's usually pointless to argue, so you just thank her enthusiastically, maybe even mentioning that they are the coolest casserole covers you've ever seen (not to mention that they're the only casserole covers you've ever seen). In the meantime, you are mulling over how you could graciously regift them and to whom you could possibly regift them. So, in the closet they go! (Along with the stainless steel pickle forks she was sure you needed last year.)

What Goes in Your Regift Closet

Now back to the stuff you have received that you actually like and (might) need. Unless you need them right away, or they are things that you could immediately display, set up, wear, use, fill, etc., you have to have a place to temporarily store them until you need them, want them, or have a place for them. All of these items can also be stored in your "Regift Closet." (Although you truly may not *intend* to ever graciously regift them, you know you should "never say, never regift.")

Stuff happens!

Labeling the appropriate shelves or areas of your "regift space" by specific item types will make it much easier to find a specific gift when you need one. Here are some label suggestions:

- **REGIFTABLES; ABSOLUTELY REGIFTABLE; REGIFTABLE ITEMS; STUFF TO REGIFT; DEFINITES**

  No-brainer gifts, i.e., stuff you don't want, would never use, can't believe you got it as a gift: **Aliens**, **TUIs**, **Freebies**, **Chronic Regifts**, etc.

- POSSIBLY REGIFTABLE; MAYBES; POTENTIAL REGIFTS; OKAY TO REGIFT

  Gifts that are sort of cool and you kind of like but would rather give to someone else; multiple gift items, like **BIBs**, **2fers**, **Promos**, **Prize Packages**, **Partial Regifts**, etc.

- PENDING; UNDECIDED; IF NEEDED; POSSIBLE KEEPERS; EXTREME EMERGENCY

  Gifts that you like and might want to keep—and might even use—but have no use for currently, but you wouldn't mind regifting in the right circumstances, like **ASOTIs**, **Collectibles**, **Do-Overs**, **Remarketers**, etc.

- NON-REGIFTABLE; KEEPERS; NOT FOR REGIFTS

  Gifts that you like, want to keep, and have no intention of regifting; stuff you will use eventually and are simply storing it; gifts you really don't want or can't use, but that absolutely *cannot / will not* be regifted…

You can come up with your own suitable categories, but keep in mind that they will probably change over time as your regiftable stock expands (or decreases), and items may move up—or down—in regiftable status.

Nevertheless, whatever storage system you choose for your regiftable stuff, *it is very important that you use a "regift log" of some sort.* Using a regift log to record the items you put into your regift storage system will ensure that you will not unintentionally commit a Regifting Faux Pas, like regifting a gift you were given to the person who originally gave you the gift (which becomes more likely the longer you keep the gift). You may even wish to note other people that were present at that particular event so that they won't receive the regift, either—unless, of course, it was something they mentioned that they would also like to have. For your convenience, there is a sample included in part 5. Feel free to copy it, or create your own, but please, for your personal "reputation protection" (and for the reputation of gracious regifting itself), you will want to utilize this form promptly for you and your regiftables, before it's too late.

How to Make (Someone) a "Regift Starter Kit"

If you are already a renowned regifter, you may currently have your share of social drawbacks, but hopefully not for long. Even so, one of the good things about it (besides probably being the neighborhood go-to person for last-minute needed gifts) is helping a friend set up their very own regifting system. What better way to introduce someone to regifting than to present him or her (no pun intended) with a Regift Starter Kit? It is easy, fun, and practical, and it serves several purposes:

1. It raises consciousness of the entire regifting concept, and the goal of a regifting revival.

2. It increases regifting knowledge while helping to prove its relevance and overall economic value.

3. And, of course, it helps to do away with some of your own regiftables in a most gratifying way.

The old "guide (them) by giving (to them)" teaching method is also a factor here. (Note: If you are a professional educator, and you have never before heard of that particular method, it's because I made it up.) In any case, here is what you need to do so that your protégé can practice regifting right away:

- Gather a few (no less than three) of your regiftables. It's okay to select ones that are less likely for you to regift, or those that you have kept for quite a while. You do not want to give up gifts that you are most likely to graciously regift sooner than later yourself.

- Figure out which of the regiftable types the items could fall under (a variety is best) and how to best regift them.

- Give him/her a copy of the Easy Regifting Reference Guide in the back of the book and jot down gracious regifting tips for each of the regiftables you have included in the kit. Ideally, you could provide them with their very own copy of this book (or regift them this one).

- Package the kit in a basket, box, bag, or any other suitable container. Using materials that you already have is another good way to point out the "recycling" benefits of regifting as well. Make a copy of one or both of the following (in part 5) and add to your kit: Regift Inventory Log Template, (Re)Gift Receipt.

- Include a copy of the Regift Starter Kit Introduction Letter with your package, and present it to your friend. When they stop jumping up and down from excitement, you can help them to get started assembling their own Regift Closet or whatever they choose to begin storing their regiftable items in.

And, voila! Another regifter is born.

Parting Words from a Regifting Goddess...

"Gracious regifting—Let someone else open it again for the first time."

~regifting proverb

Believe it or not, every one of the recognized gift types discussed in part 3 has actually been received, and/or given, within my family. Likewise, at one time or another, these items have been graciously regifted using one of the methods or examples described. (Although, not necessarily within my family!) Every experience here is true; however, the names have been changed to protect the ignorant. However, many of the examples have been somewhat altered to avoid any kind of fallout from my family and friends, as well as any other unsuspecting regift getters.

Let's face it—we have become a generation of greed. We want what we want, we want the best, and we want it fast but with minimum effort. Although regifting is a highly reputable and reasonable way to give really great gifts, there will probably always be people who choose to call us "cheaters" and chide us for being "cheap." It is most unfortunate that there are some who feel that the "value" of a gift is relative to its cost, and that the cost of the gift is proportional to the significance of the relationship itself. However, most of us still prefer—at least halfway, anyway—to simply be appreciated for the act of our gracious gift giving, regardless of whether the gift was a regift. We give because we want to. We regift because we can. We graciously regift because we care. Quite frankly, there is no greater gift (whether it be a regift, or not) than that.

A regifting revival will help to alleviate a lot of the "Just Plain Lazy" and "Really Lame" labels given to regifters, as well as make gracious regifting much more acceptable to the average gift giver, and gift getter. Instead of being labeled "losers," Gracious Regifters should now be regarded as environmentalists! Gracious regifting will be redeemed and be revolutionized as a responsible way to recycle our unwanted gifts! Regifters everywhere will finally be awarded the respect and admiration we so definitely deserve!

Crusading for a Real Regifting Revival

Of course, this regifting revival can only become a reality if everyone willingly does his or her part in personally helping to convince others *to actively participate*—repeatedly—in the practice of gracious regifting. It has to be talked up! It has to take off! It has to become big! Gracious regifting must grow into a popular gift-giving alternative for almost all people, no matter how pretentious, rich, poor, or practical they may be!

But keep in mind that, for regifting to go mainstream, we must also be willing to put aside our prejudices toward the people who still insist that regifting is the uneducated choice of little kids, losers, procrastinators, and cheapskates! We strongly recommend that you do us all a favor, please, and give these people a copy of this gracious regifting guide. In fact, you can even lend or regift *this* copy after you have finished reading it yourself!

If you really want to go grass roots for gracious regifting and actively campaign for its eventual comeback, then you will want to get busy! Make magnets, hang banners, stick up signs, furnish flyers, and wear T-shirts, buttons, and badges to display your fervor, your commitment, and your dedication to this incredibly important cause! Gather your family, friends, neighbors, and co-workers and enlist their support! Provide them with this book! And then give these items to your guests, pin them on your patients, and clip them to your customers and clients. Staple them to your students (just kidding). You can even attach them to your animals (except for the pins, please). Put them on your purse, wear one on your wallet, plus keep a couple on your keychain. However and wherever you decide to don them, and whatever you decide to do, please do not give up on our goal for all of the Gracious Regifters everywhere to

Make Gracious Regifting the Right Way

To Always Recycle

The Wrong Gifts You Get!

"A regift is better than no gift."

~regifting proverb

5 The Regifting Tool Kit

Gracious Regifting FAQ

To assist you in your role in helping to make a regifting revival an absolute reality, and to help gracious regifting begin to happen in every household, we have come up with a quick Q&A to hopefully nip some of your initial regifting questions in the bud and to help you answer questions posed by as yet anti-regifters.

Q. Can an item be regifted more than once?

A. Yes, indeed. In fact, some gifts are actually intended to be regifted repeatedly, like the **Perpetual Present**. To keep it simple, however, and to avoid mass confusion, it does not need to be referred to as a re-regift or a re-re-regift, regift[2], etc. We will just presume that any time a gift is given again to another gift getter, it is referred to as a regift, no matter how many times the same gift has been regifted. (If you are planning to regift a regift, if possible, try to alter or embellish it in some way to keep it from looking "tired" or used. You still want the gift to be appropriate and be appreciated by the gift getter, no matter how many times it may have been regifted.)

Q. Can a gift be "partially used" and still be regifted?

A. There is "partially used" as in a gift you or someone else has already opened and used all or part of at some time after they got it (e.g., the **Collectible**, the **Do-over**, and the **Fab Find**). As long as the item is still "as good as new," you can graciously regift it, but probably not to just anyone. If "partially used" means that you want to keep part of the gift, but regift the rest, that's okay, too. Refer to the **2fer** and the **Partial Gift** for examples. You can also give a "partial regift" as the term is defined in Regift Exception #3.

Q. Can you personalize a gift you want to regift to someone?

A. Certainly, and it makes sense, especially if the gift could be more appreciated if it was embellished with the gift getter's name, initials, or some sort of slogan or mantra that they often use. Other ways to "personalize" a potential regift could be in the unique or creative way that you repackage it. (See the section in part 4 "Think Outside the (Regift) Box" for more ideas.)

Q. If you suspect you have been given a regift, or it is obvious because the original "to/from" card was still enclosed, do you mention it?

A.   This is a tricky one. How you choose to handle this situation strongly depends on the kind of relationship you have with the gift giver. In most cases, it is probably best to keep mum about it, extol your gratitude, and, if necessary, regift it yourself, especially if you only *suspect* it is a regift. If you are sure that the gift giver has a good sense of humor and would find their faux pas pretty funny and not feel at all humiliated, then go ahead and tell them, but certainly not in a mean-spirited manner. And certainly still show your appreciation for the giving gesture.

Q. What if you receive a gift that has to be assembled, and once you do, you decide it is not something that you would like but it would make a good regift. Should you regift it already assembled, or should you disassemble it and carefully put it back in the original box to regift it?

A.   You can go either way with this, and it depends on who you plan to give it to, and how complicated it is to put together. If the item is fairly simple to assemble, and it's easy to tell what it is (by the picture on the box if there is one), then you might want to regift it back in the box. However, if the gift's construction is rather complicated, or it's difficult to tell what it is while in pieces, then regifting it intact is probably a better idea, especially if it is being graciously regifted to children or elderly folks.

Q. If you bought something for yourself, your spouse, or child and, for whatever reason, after you got it home you changed your mind about it (and were too lazy or too late to return it), is it still considered regifting if you decide to give it to someone else, even if it's never been opened and/or used?

A.   If you simply give the item to someone else for no particular occasion, and you explain it as "I got this for myself, but I decided I didn't need it. Do you want it?" then it is not a regift. However, if you actually give the item to someone as a gift as in a special occasion where giving a gift is expected, and without disclosing the circumstances in which you got it, e.g., "Happy Birthday, I thought you would love this," it is regifting. Even if you give the unwanted item to someone *as a gift* and express it as such, e.g., "I got this for myself but changed my mind and figured you would really like it," then it is still a regift. (See Regift Exception #2.)

Q. If you lead or manage a staff where gifts and prizes are frequently given, as incentives and rewards, is it ethical to use your own regiftable items?

A. Most definitely! In fact, using your own stash of regiftable stuff for prizes and incentives for your staff is a terrific way to recycle them and to set a good example of your ecological commitment to your employees! Of course, it is still very important to review the "Faux Pas" section in part 4 again, as well as the appropriate gracious regifting tips for the individual items, unless you are not worried about being discreet. However, if that is the case, you will need to be wary of anyone who may be getting a regift as his or her prize who would not find it the least bit resourceful and may actually be insulted. (Naturally, these very same people need to be assured that, in fact, gracious regifting is now considered perfectly normal and really quite necessary. If you are a supervisor, you might even want to suggest that any staff person who is seen purposely snubbing the practice of gracious regifting in the office does not have to participate in the incentive program. The harassment of gracious regifting in the workplace will no longer be tolerated!)

Q. Are items purchased from a pawnshop, estate sale, or through an online store such as eBay, and then given as gifts considered regifts?

A. If there is some sort of "proof" that the item is actually brand-new, complete with tags or original packaging, then it is not a regift. (Unless it is included with another regift. See Regift Exception #3.) However, if there is no such proof, or if you are not sure, then you would consider it a regift and graciously regift it as such. (See Regift Exception #2.)

Q. If there is truly going to be a regifting revival, and people everywhere really become more capable and confident in gracious regifting, shouldn't we also then be just as accepting and appreciative of *getting* a regift from someone, no matter how graciously—or not—it is given to us?

A. Yes, certainly! Naturally, if we are going to feel good about graciously regifting to those getting a gift from us, then we should feel equally as pleased to receive a recycled gift from someone else, especially since that is one less unwanted gift that might otherwise have been wasted. (This could result in a **Chronic Regift** gifting cycle, or maybe a **Perpetual Present**.)

Q. What can I, an average (or below average) gift giver, do *right now* for my part in helping to get the regifting revival off the ground, and to be successful in seriously reducing the amount of unwanted gift waste currently clogging up our closets and storage units?

A. An excellent question, indeed! The first thing, of course, is to make sure that everyone you know has access to the important information contained in this book. And don't just "talk the talk." You really have to "regift the gift"—whenever the opportunity presents itself (no pun intended). Lead by example! Take that bull by the horns and graciously regift it! Help people everywhere to understand that an unwanted gift is a terrible thing to waste, so you just gotta graciously regift it.

Giving a Gift to a Frequent Regifter

When you are an experienced regifter (admittedly, I have been referred to as the Regifting Queen; however, I personally prefer to refer to myself as a Regifting Goddess…!), there is rarely any gift-giving situation that you are unable to deal with appropriately. However, there are a few social drawbacks to being so gifted, no pun intended. No matter how capable you are in giving great gifts, as well as being uniquely qualified in gracious regifting techniques, you do tend to acquire a reputation of sorts. People who are aware of your fondness for regifting often have a problem deciding what kinds of gifts to give you that you will not be apt to regift. It becomes a personal challenge for them to be able to come up with and give an "unregiftable" gift. Sometimes they can be inclined to really dwell on the subject for a number of reasons, all of which are totally bogus! Soon it won't matter anyway because everyone will be agreeable to gracious regifting. But until that happens:

1. They figure that no matter what gift they give you, or why, you will probably eventually regift it.

2. You will never be completely honest about a particular gift that you got, no matter how much you said you liked it (and then you will most likely go ahead and regift it).

3. No matter what kind of gift that you get, you will be wondering how to regift it and who to regift it to within moments of receiving it.

Not to mention that presumably any gift you give to someone is probably also a regift. Although no one is actually complaining about receiving any of your most-likely-regifted presents, there are still some feelings of uncertainty in any gift-giving or gift-getting situation that you are a part of.

Apparently, these people are paranoid. They are suffering from G.A.S. (Gift Apprehension Syndrome). This can be a very serious affliction among those that give to and/or get gifts from frequent regifters. It could possibly affect friendships and family relationships if it is not soon corrected and/or dealt with accordingly. We definitely do not want this to become epidemic.

The perception that you could not sincerely appreciate a gift given to you by anyone, and that any gift you give is a regift, is somewhat insulting, to say the least. So for all of you gift givers who are in a quandary as to what, or how, to give a great gift to an accomplished regifter, here are a few ideas for guaranteed-to-please gifts worth giving:

1. Cash—preferably in large bills.

2. Okay, just kidding with number one (although it certainly would be a guaranteed non-regift). However, you can always resort again to the "chicken choice" of a favored gift card (still not a 100 percent guarantee against regifting).

3. A gift that is truly something the giftee has requested and not a "reasonable facsimile" (read cheap substitute).

4. Travel gifts (e.g., an Alaskan Cruise) are always welcome and appreciated.

5. For something less pretentious, movie, concert, or theater tickets are a good bet if you are in tune with your giftee's taste in "The Arts." Buying one for them and one for you is a good excuse to absorb some culture as well.

6. A "sophisticated" gag gift (my personal favorite). This is a gift that usually contains a number of items, generally relating to a specific theme, e.g., "A Party in a Box" filled with a fun assortment of party stuff, favors, etc. One of the best gifts I ever got was a unique collection of "The Lamest Gifts Ever." Despite that almost every one of the items included in this gift could have, and definitely would have been, regifted under any other circumstances—probably as TUIs—the idea that each lame gift had been carefully selected for

the theme, and that it included a hilarious letter explaining the whole thing, made it very special.

(See, that isn't so hard, now is it?)

Easy Regifting Reference Guide

Types of gift givers

- **Generous:** *always giving gifts* for any reason
- **Gratuitous:** gives gifts *out of a sense of obligation*
- **Forgetful:** gives gifts *at the last minute*
- **Grudging:** *hates giving gifts* and wasting money

Types of gift getters

- **Genial:** *loves every gift* no matter what
- **Grateful:** *overwhelming thanks* for everything
- **Greedy:** *always disappointed* in amount, never enough
- **Grumbling:** *complains unappreciatively* about every gift

Gift Types To Regift

SUPER SIMPLE: needs no enhancement

1. **The Alien** (*What is it? What's it for?*)

2. **The ASOTI** (*As Seen On TV Item — "But wait, there's more…"*)

3. **The BIB** (*Bought In Bulk*)

4. **The Collectible** (*excessive additions, also "heirlooms"*)

5. **The Perpetual Present** (*purposely regifted repeatedly*)

6. **The Prize Package** (*won as a prize*)

FAIRLY EASY: needs minimal enhancement

7. **The 2fer** (*multiple items split into two or more gifts*)

8. **The BOGO** (*Buy One Get One Free items, free with purchase*)

9. **The Partial Gift** (*keep part of gift, regift the rest*)

10. **The Upscaler** (*"cheap" item regifted in "lavish" packaging*)

A. **The Gift Card**

B. **Food Items**

C. **Seasonal Stuff** (*holiday- and special occasion-themed gifts*)

D. **Jewelry**

E. **Clothing and Shoes**

🎁 🎁 🎁 A TAD TRICKY: needs some enhancement, add-ons, or repackaging and creativity

11. **The Freebie** (*given out at events or from VIPs*)

12. **The Souvenir** (*from tourist shops, airports, special places*)

F. **Books**

G. **Perfumes, Colognes, Body Sprays, etc.**

H. **Toys**

I. **Video games, CDs, and DVDs**

🎁 🎁 🎁 🎁 DIFFICULT: not for the novice; needs combination of add-ons, embellishments, repackaging, and a *lot* of creativity and imagination

13. **The Do-Over** (*old gift / purchased used*)

14. **The IDer** (*name or moniker on it*)

15. **The Promo** (*branded with company, business logo*)

J. **Power Tools, Electronics, and Small Appliances**

16. **The Chronic Regift** (*no one wants it*)

17. **The Fab Find** (*found somewhere and not bought*)

18. **The Remarketer** (*intended for other use*)

19. **The TUI** (*Totally Useless Item*)

K. **Plants and Flowers**

The Fundamentals of Gracious Regifting

Gracious Regifting Fundamental #1: Gracious regifting is the subtle art of reusing gifts that you have previously received by giving them as gifts to someone else in such a genuine, creative, and clever manner that they are still considered to be friendly, tasteful, and favorable.

Gracious Regifting Fundamental #2: Almost *any* gift received can be regifted, but not all gifts can be regifted in just *any* way!

Gracious Regifting Fundamental #3: It really can be better to give than to receive. (Just as long as you don't try to deceive.) It is even better to regift—graciously, of course!

Gracious Regifting Fundamental #4: As a Gracious Regifter, it is good practice to always give a regift better than how you received it.

Regift Exception #1: If something has been sitting in storage over a period of time with no particular gift getter in mind, or if any of the products were purchased with the intention of giving them as gifts at some point, then it becomes a "generic regift" and is graciously regifted accordingly.

Regift Exception #2: If an item made, found, or purchased was at some point previously used by, or intended for, yourself or anyone else, and you decide to give it as a gift to someone else, it is still regarded as a regift.

Regift Exception #3: If a newly purchased item is given as part of a gift along with a regiftable item, or a regiftable item is part of a gift that also includes a newly purchased item, whether simply for add-on or enhancement purposes, the entire gift is still considered a regift.

Ways to Clean out the Regift Closet

Okay, since you are now beginning to store regiftable items, you will eventually acquire an enormous selection of suitable (and some unsuitable) regift items in your storage system. This could make future shopping for a new gift almost futile, and unnecessary. Without a doubt, you will have the perfect present for nearly anyone, and some (questionably?) unique gifts for your (lucky?) friends and family. From now on, absolutely no gift-giving occasion or opportunity will need to be avoided due to your lack of appropriate treasures.

But what if the holidays are far away and there are no birthday parties beckoning? Or if, sadly, not a single relevant event is marked on your cal-

endar anytime soon, either? What do you do if you have lots of great gifts to graciously regift, but no giftees to get them? Well, when one is faced with this sort of unusual situation, there are several different options for cleaning out your regift closet that you may not have thought of:

- You could give some (appropriate) items to schools, organizations, and other places that are soliciting donations and merchandise to use as prizes and gift items for fund-raising events, e.g., church bingo, PTA raffles, theme baskets, silent auctions, and senior care centers. Doing so will make you feel all warm and fuzzy inside, regardless of whether or not you get the tax deduction. (Usually they will take almost anything…)

- If you are interested in raising money for a favorite charity, or some type of "fun"draising idea, how about setting up an "Awful Item Auction"? Have folks wrap up one or more of their unwanted gifts in some creative, original way and donate them to be auctioned off. Since they are already packaged, no one will really know what exactly that they are bidding on, but it's all in good fun (and hopefully for a good cause). You could also set it up as a "KISS" silent auction (Kontinually Inventing Stupid Stuff). No one has to wrap or repackage anything and you have fun with the item descriptions, making them clever or corny. (And, quite likely, everyone will end up with at least one other "new" regiftable item...)

- You could choose to use them for goodies and prizes for your own parties and contests.

- You plan a regifting party! A "Regift Gala" or a "Regift Exchange"! The core concept of this exciting event would be some version of the White Elephant game. For your party, "Steal the Regift" will require that everyone you invite brings a regiftable item, whether already gifted once before or not (your choice!). You might want to consider giving prizes (from your own regifts, of course) for the best, oddest, tackiest, and most ridiculous regiftable gift that was received (or one they regifted). You could expand this party plan and really go crazy coming up with some very interesting and inventive ideas, e.g., invitations written on already-received greeting cards, flyers, etc. Everyone could bring leftovers for the eats, or better yet, a food gift they have (recently) received. Having a regifting party would definitely be a wild and wacky way to

- provide a fun, social—and functional—party for your friends, and their regiftables;

- get rid of some of your regiftable overstock, while also allowing others to thin out their regift-worthy things;

- refamiliarize your guests with the concept of regifting, and promote the new and improved practice of proper and gracious regifting; and

- pass out regifting revival propaganda! Give out regift goody bags!

The Regift Starter Kit Introduction Letter

A copy of the following letter can be added to or given with the Regift Starter Kit. You may also want to include a copy of the (Re)gift Receipt, Regift Inventory Log Template, and an Easy Regifting Reference Guide. Feel free to add anything else you feel would be helpful.

Welcome, New Regifter!

Congratulations! You have just been given a great gift! This gift will get you started on being able to give others great gifts, too—gifts that you have already gotten. Regifts!

These tools, along with some "training," will help you to become more than just a regifter. You will soon learn and understand how to reuse your unwanted gifts *graciously*. Gracious regifting is a higher level of regifting: classy and more refined. You will be able to proudly give anyone a gift that was previously given to you in clever ways you never thought possible!

In your kit, you have _____ of the different gift types that are typically regifted and some helpful tips on how to graciously regift each. You may have given or gotten some of these types of gifts yourself at one time. The next time you do, you'll know just what you can do with them, and with many of the other gifts you'll be getting in the future. Now, no gift will ever be wasted, and almost every unwanted gift can be graciously regifted, including the ones in here!

Of course, you may keep these gifts for yourself, if you would like. They are yours to use or do with whatever you want. However, you may want to consider using these gifts as "practice presents" to hone your regifting skills. Then, whenever the need arises for you to give someone a gift and you feel you already have something that is suitable, you will be ready to graciously regift it! More importantly, gracious regifting will become yet another fine option in your future gift-giving arsenal. Not only will you be conserving your cash, and other valuable resources, you will also be recycling gifts that would otherwise be wasted. That is why gracious regifting is not only good for you, and for your giftees, but it's also very good for the environment. And that's good for everyone!

Remember: Almost *any* gift received can be regifted, but not every gift can be regifted in just *any* way!

The (Re)Gift Receipt

If gracious regifting is going to become just another acceptable way to give someone a gift without carrying any negative connotation, then we also have to be comfortable with the notion that there will be a time when a gift we have given someone will possibly get regifted, no matter how carefully it was chosen. On the other hand, if you are in doubt for any reason about the gift you are about to give, then the receipt on the back of this page may be welcome. You may want to begin including one with all of the gifts that you give, since that is another way to positively promote the practical benefits of regifting, even if the gift you are giving is already a regift.

You may want to personalize it for your gift getter.

🎁 (RE)GIFT RECEIPT 🎁

This gift was selected especially for you in celebration for this occasion.

    This (Re)Gift Receipt has been given to you, along with your gift, to allow you the option to graciously regift this to anyone else, should you choose to do so, for any reason whatsoever, without guilt or shame.

    Please feel free to pass this present on to another person under any circumstances, should they seem appropriate. Or, you may simply regift it to someone else whom you assume would be more appreciative. You are not under any obligation to inform me of your decision, as it is a gift for you and therefore yours to do with whatever you wish. I assure you that no matter what, I will still always be:

(Fill In the blank) _____

The Regift Inventory Log Template

In order to keep accurate records of your gifts, thus avoiding any unnecessary embarrassment, or hard feelings among friends and family, it is a good idea to keep a log such as the following to use in your regift closet, or wherever you store your regiftables. Use this handy form, or create one of your own. Feel free to personalize it and/or make any adjustments needed for your own system.

Regifting Record

Gift	Received From/Date	Regifted To/Date	Notes

🎁 Regifting Record 🎁

Gift	Received From/Date	Regifted To/Date	Notes

✿ *Regifting Record* ✿

Gift	Received From/ Date	Regifted To/Date	Notes

Acknowledgments

Much appreciation goes to my family and my assortment of wonderful friends, not only for providing me with an unlimited amount of gifts and material for this book throughout the years, but for also providing me with an unlimited amount of love and support.

Thanks to Amanda and Kevin, our God-sent blessings, who, among other things, inspire me to be better. And especially thanks to my husband, Larry, who, along with his unconditional love, support, and encouragement, kept his boot up my backside while always believing in this book, and in us.

A special thanks to Doris, my friend and neighbor, who, after admitting her lack of regifting knowledge, inspired me to write the "original" ten-page "A Gift Giver's Guide to Gracious Regifting: How To Give What You Have Received." I included a "FREE Starter Kit!" and gave it to her as a Christmas gift several years ago. You have to start somewhere!

Many thanks to everyone who then had input, ideas, and advice while encouraging me to make it into a "real book" and start a regifting comeback. (Especially you, Angie.)

Thanks also to the outstanding team at BookPros, who helped make this idea a reality; especially to those who *so patiently* dealt with my ignorance, anxieties, poor punctuation, ghastly grammar, excessively long sentences, and my annoying alliterations. (You know who you are!) I can proudly claim that I have given new meaning to the editing term "passive voice…" and won awards for my frequent fragmented sentences and incredible repeated usage of severely split infinitives. You guys are the best!

(And I should probably also thank Jerry *Seinfeld*, who first coined and popularized the term "regift" in a classic episode of *Seinfeld*, a TV series that was faithfully watched by myself, most of my friends, and my then "twenty-thirty something" roommates, who could totally relate. "This book is for you.")